DUMFRIES

FOLK
TALES

DUMFRIES & GALLOWAY

FOLK TALES

TONY BONNING

ILLUSTRATED BY JO JACKSON BONNING

To the memory of my inspirational parents and grandparents
Chick, Babs, Geordie and Bessie

– Tony Bonning

Dedicated to my wonderful son Maxim
and dearest parents Ken and Mary

– Jo Jackson Bonning

First published 2016

The History Press
The Mill, Brimscombe Port
Stroud, Gloucestershire, GL5 2QG
www.thehistorypress.co.uk

Reprinted 2017

British Library Cataloguing in Publication Data.
A catalogue record for this book is available from the British Library.

ISBN 978 0 7509 6840 9

Typesetting and origination by The History Press
Printed in Great Britain by TJ Books Ltd, Padstow, Cornwall.

CONTENTS

About the Author

Tony Bonning was born into a Scots-speaking farming family in South-West Scotland in 1948. He is a bestselling author, top storyteller and versatile singer and musician, and does over two hundred shows a year for children as his alter-ego, Aiken Drum. He is founder of the Galloway Children's Festival, co-founder and play leader of the Play-it-by-Ear music groups and co-founder of the national poetry magazine, *Markings*. He was also part of the group that established the Wickerman Festival in 2002 and ran the Children's Area for thirteen years. In his spare time he goes hill-walking with his wife Jo to write poetry. Tony has seven children and one god-daughter.

ABOUT THE ILLUSTRATOR

Jo Jackson Bonning was born and raised in the Cotswolds and has one son called Maxim. Jo and Maxim moved to Kirkcudbright in South-West Scotland seventeen years ago when her son was four to be nearer to her parents Ken, an Ayrshire man, and Mary Jackson, who also live in Kirkcudbright. In her early twenties, Jo gained distinction in her studies of textile design in Derbyshire and completed her art training at Goldsmith's College in London in 1985/6. After her move to Scotland, Jo attended Strathclyde University to train to be a drama teacher and is currently teaching drama at Kirkcudbright Academy. Jo has greatly enjoyed illustrating her husband Tony's book, especially as it is their first collaboration which has united both their areas of great interest: storytelling and art.

INTRODUCTION

In 1846, Professor William Thom coined the term 'folklore', a much better and succinct description than the previous 'popular antiquities'. This was the period when the serious study of folk beliefs, folk tales, legends and myths was put under scientific scrutiny. The major advantage was that the tales that were the entertainment and the education of people were collected by people like the Brothers Grimm in Germany, Charles Perrault in France, and Robert Chambers and J.F. Campbell in Scotland. This meant that the tales were preserved as books became more readily available. The downside was that literacy spelled the end of oral culture. Over the last twenty-odd years there has been a great revival in storytelling in Scotland and across Britain as a whole, not that it really ever went away, especially among the traveller community. I was fortunate that both my paternal grandmother and grandfather regaled me with tales, as did my mother. My grandfather, whom I lived with and cared for in his later years, would happily tell tales all through the night. In his world, the barrier between fact and fiction was often blurred, and was all the better for it.

For the past fifty years I have been fascinated by the history, culture and lore of Scotland's South-West. It all began with curiosity at the Gaelic place names. At the age of twelve I cycled through a place blessed with the wonderful name of Clachaneasy. It took a while, but eventually I discovered that *clachan* was the Gaelic for 'village' or 'settlement' and *easy* was from *Iosa*, the Gaelic for Jesus. If you will excuse the dreadful cliché, I was now a man (or was that, boy) on a mission. The greatest realisation was that behind every name was a story filled with history, culture, geography and people. One could look at a place in four, perhaps five dimensions. It was, and is, exhilarating.

Dumfries and Galloway is 6,426 square kilometres – roughly 140 kilometres (eighty-eight miles) wide and seventy kilometres (forty-four miles) at its deepest. It comprises pastoral lowland, upland and mountains. It is divided into Dumfries to the east and Galloway to the west. Rivers play a big part in delineating the region. Furthest east is Eskdale then Annadale with Nithsdale as the west side of Dumfries. Galloway formerly began at the Nith but the area along the west bank of the Nith is now subsumed by the Dumfries area of Nithsdale. Between there and the river Cree is the Stewartry of Kirkcudbright and from the Cree to Portpatrick is Wigtownshire. Because of geography, Galloway was always a land unto itself and as a result there are many tales that are unique to the area. It was heavily influenced by connections with Ireland and the Norse-Gael – the Gall-Ghaedheil, who most likely gave the region its name. East of the Nith, Dumfriesshire had more of a Border influence, though many place names have a decidedly Norse ring to them. East of the Nith there are the Faery Folk – the Guid Neichbours; west of the Nith they are the Daoine Sith.

I have done my best to balance the tales according to place, but in the end the deciding factor was whether it was a good tale. The whole region has many hundreds of stories, many of which are similar, changing to suit time and place and the persuasions of the teller, and I have shown a bit of that in the tales herein. I hope you enjoy the selection.

The book could have been made easier by having everyone speaking in standard English. I have chosen not to for a number of reasons. Firstly, I was born into a Scots-speaking farming family in the South-West and it is my first language – it was thrashed out of me and my fellow pupils at school. We have a word for that nowadays: it's called racism – not to mention elitism and classism. The people of the times these tales relate to spoke Scots and I feel this must be respected – many of the original written tales were wholly in Scots and are a difficult read, even for many modern

Scots. With this in mind I have narrated in standard English but left most dialogue in the old tongue, with current Scots spelling. The one thing not changed, to avoid confusion, is 'I', which in Scots is pronounced as 'A'. Preserving our language is vital to our culture. Even if we don't use it generally, we should at least have a good grounding in it; otherwise we lose something of our national soul. At first, the language may seem difficult and there are many words not in English usage, but if you read the passage aloud the meaning will often become clear. If not, there is a fairly complete glossary at the end, so please take the time to use it.

Lastly, Jo and I would like to thank all those who have contributed to the making of this volume, in particular Lesley Garbutt and Russell Bryden of Kirkcudbright Library, for their enormous help over many years. Bless you.

Tony Bonning, 2016

1

RASHIE COAT

Langholm, or the *Muckle Toun*, as it is locally known, is an attractive small town set among wooded hills on the banks of the River Esk. It is most famous for its woollen mills and is the birthplace of one of Scotland's greatest poets, Hugh MacDiarmid (real name Christopher Grieve).

Long ago, the Laird and Lady of Langholm had a beautiful and gifted daughter whom they named Ella. As a young girl, her mother had shown her how to weave and spin and knit and sow and in each of these arts she became highly proficient. Her mother also walked with her through the woods that clad the hills along the banks of the Esk and filled her with a sense of wonder at all the gifts of nature. One day her mother cut some thin willow wands, formed them into a hoop through which she wove leaves and flowers. She then placed this rustic crown on her daughter's head. 'You have always been my princess, but now you are the Princess of Langholm.' So awed by her mother's creation was she that in time she learned how to weave grasses, plant stems and willow wands into dresses, shoes and other garments. Her finest creation was a coat made from the rushes that grew by the river; from this she was often called Rashie Coat.

It was winter's end when her mother died. Rashie Coat was so distressed that she gave up on worldly things to the point where she would wear the same clothes day in, day out. She slept by the fireside and barely ate. Her distraught father, not knowing what to do, decided that it was best if she was married. This was quite the last thing she wanted to do. Besides, her mother had married for love and she would do nothing less. On the other hand, she did not wish to offend her loving father; he too had lost the person he loved most in the world besides her. Not knowing what to do, she decided to visit the hen-wife who lived at the bottom of the garden. The hen-wife looked after the hens, ducks and geese of the laird. Like all hen-wives she possessed some second sight. Not professionally like a spae-wife or dangerously like a witch, but more in the way of everyday wisdom.

'Come in miss,' said the hen-wife. 'It is indeed a pleesure tae hae ye veesit oor humble cot. Whit can we dae fer ye?'

Rashie Coat stepped inside to be met with the sharp stink of hen droppings. She was about to step back out but decided it would be insulting. The woman proffered a chair that had a few badly wiped marks on it. Seeing the offending poop, the woman wiped it with her pinafore then proffered the seat again. 'It's alright, thank you. I've been sitting all day and could do with a bit of standing. Anyway, I wanted to ask your advice.' The woman cocked her head to the side, the better to hear. 'My father wishes me to be married, but I have no desire to wed just yet. Especially not to the sop my father has chosen. I don't wish to sound mean.' The hen-wife shook her head in agreement. Rashie Coat gave a sigh, 'He's nice enough, but just not right. What should I do?'

The hen-wife called her daughter from the garden. The girl was a big-boned, country lass with red hair partially hidden under a mutch; she too had her mother's hen-like mannerisms and kept nodding her head as if she was about to peck. 'Get me a bowl o watter frae the spring,' said the mother. The girl took a wooden bowl from the rickety dresser and went out. The woman made small talk until the girl returned, then she set the bowl on a three-legged stool, bent her knees at right angles to each other and began to circle the stool making a soft, clucking sound. She then stopped and her head shot forward as if she was about to take a drink. Her nose stopped an inch from the water. She gazed into it then shot upright. 'Ye maun insist that ye get a coat o beaten gowd afore ye will mairry the mannie.'

Rashie Coat gave the woman a bawbee as payment and went straight to her father and asked if he would get her a coat of beaten gold so that she might marry the suitor. Her father went into his vaults and removed a box of gold coins. These he took to his goldsmith and asked him to make a coat of beaten gold. Although the man had never made any such thing before he set to work and made an exquisite garment that not only shimmered with light but seemed to flow like silk. Rashie Coat was delighted and thought it the most beautiful thing she had ever seen as she swayed back and forth listening to the swish of the gold sheet. Her father stood and admired how beautiful his daughter looked dressed in this fine raiment. 'Now can we arrange a day for your wedding?'

Rashie Coat stopped swaying and stood for a moment looking at the floor, 'I can't marry him, Father.' She let the coat fall and ran from the room and made her way to the hen-wife, 'What am I to do?'

Again the hen-wife sent her daughter for water, again she strutted round the bowl, peered into it, leaped up and proclaimed, 'Ye maun ask yer faither tae get ye a coat made frae feathers o aa the burds o the air.' Rashie Coat gave the woman a bawbee and went to see her father again.

Her father shook his head in amazement, 'Do you not like your coat of beaten gold?'

'I love the coat, but if I am to marry the suitor I must had a decent wardrobe.'

'So be it!' her father said in resignation. He called a retainer and ordered him to collect a bag of grain and ask the birds of the air if they would give a feather in exchange for a beak-full of the cereal. Always glad of a free meal, birds came from far and wide, dropped a feather and made off with their fee. The laird's tailor then zealously stitched every feather to a coat of the finest silk brocade. The laird was highly impressed with the coat, as was his daughter, though her face looked glum. 'You don't like it?' asked her father in surprise.

'I love it but it has not convinced me that I should marry.' She saw the look of frustration and rising anger in her father's face. 'Be a little patient. There's something I need to do.' With this she left swiftly and made her way to the hen-wife's door. 'I'm sorry if I'm wasting your time but I still can't bring myself to marry the suitor. What shall I do?'

'Come in and we'll see whit the seein bowl sees.' The hen-wife went through her ritual and again leaped up and said, 'Ye maun get a coat and shoon made frae rashes.'

'But I have shoes and a coat made of rushes.'

'Aye missy, I ken that. But they, an aa yer claes, are bonny things and ye need something that is mair ... shall we say, humble: something like kintra-fowk wear.' Rashie Coat gave the woman another bawbee and set off to see her father.

'Why would you want such a thing?' he protested, 'Why not silk and fine grain leather?'

'It's what I need before I can consent to marry,' she answered.

Her father sent for his best woodsman who, together with his wife, artfully made shoes and a coat that fitted Rashie Coat exactly. The laird was not impressed, 'I have to admit they are well made, but they are not what I would expect a daughter of mine to wear; the coat you made was better. I said nothing at the time because you had made it and because your mother loved it, but it was not exactly becoming of a young lady. Now you really are Rashie Coat.' He gave a long exasperated sigh, then taking her head in his hands he looked down at her with pleading eyes, 'The wedding?'

Rashie Coat slowly took off the shoes and the coat and looked up into her father's kind and loving eyes and, with her heart near breaking and tears welling, said, 'I can't. I just can't.' She turned and fled from the room. Dropping the coat and shoes at the back door the girl ran into the garden and down to the hen-wife's little cottage. She banged on the door and incautiously opened it. 'Hen-wife, are you there?'

'Whit can I dae fer ye, young miss?'

The voice from behind made her jump and step back awkwardly into some mud at the side of the door. There was also a tone in the voice that unsettled Rashie Coat. 'Oh! What a fright you gave me.'

'Sorry aboot that.' The apology came over as insincere, 'Noo whit can I dae fer ye?'

'I still can't go through with the wedding. What can I do?'

'I dinnae ken miss; there's nae ither wey I can help ye. I hae duin ma best by ye. Noo by yer leave I hae tae get on wi feedin the chookies.' She turned and walked away, leaving Rashie Coat with a feeling of helplessness.

Not knowing what else to do, Rashie Coat returned to her house and put on an old, plain dress along with the coat and shoes made of rushes. She then took the coat of beaten gold, the coat of many feathers and light slippers along with some apples and a chunk of bread and put them in a wicker basket. She strapped it to her back and slipped out of the house. It was just past midday, so using the sun as reference Rashie Coat headed westwards towards Lockerbie, some eighteen miles away, reaching it just before seven. Feeling that she was still too close to home, she spent the night at the base of a haystack before heading further west to Dumfries. There she found her way to a large imposing house in the centre of town and knocked on a side door. The middle-aged woman who answered seemed put out with the interruption, 'What dae ye want?' the woman asked brusquely.

'I am a guid wirker and wondered if ye had ony wark ye needed daein?' Ella said, disguising her upbringing.

'Ye cam at the richt time; I hae juist feenisht aff a lass. I'll show ye the scullery and ye can get on wi the dishes.' The woman showed her the kitchen and the scullery, as well as the pallet that would now be her bed.

After Rashie Coat had finished the mountain of dishes, thrown out the dirty water and refilled the pots to heat the water for the next set of dishes, she set about clearing up the mess of ashes left by the last servant lass. In no time she had transformed the scullery and tidied up the kitchen, which pleased the cooks. She was a diligent worker and soon was popular with the other servants, though she was inclined to keep her own company. On Saturday afternoon, whilst she was helping the cooks with shopping in the mercat, she noticed a bookshop and, asking her leave for a few

minutes, went inside and purchased a book of poetry. That night she sat with a candle reading and memorising the poems. Next day was Sunday and the laird, his wife, daughters, son and staff set out for church. Rashie Coat was left at home to make sure the dinner was hot on their return. She was blowing the fire to get it going when she was aware of a presence in the room. She turned and almost fell back into the inglenook in fright. Before her was the apparition of a woman. She wore a long gossamer dress, not unlike one her mother used to wear. Rashie Coat could not make out the face from the bright light that shone around it, but she noticed a circlet about the head decorated with leaves and flowers. 'Don't be afraid,' the phantom said kindly. 'Today is the Sabbath and not a day for work. Put on your coat of beaten gold and go to church.'

'But I have to make sure dinner is hot and ready for the laird's return.'

'Be assured that on your return the dinner will be just perfect. Now go!'

Rashie Coat put on the coat of beaten gold and as she did the grimy, unkempt servant-look disappeared and she blossomed into the beauty she truly was. As she opened the door to leave she extemporised a rhyme:

Ae *peat* gar *anither peat burn,*	one, make
Ae spit gar anither spit turn,	
Ae pat *gar anither pat play,*	pot
Let Rashie Coat gang *tae the kirk the day.*	go

With a smile and a wave she set out for Greyfriars Church. On the way she realised she had not asked the apparition who she was: a guardian angel, a fairy godmother or a guid neichbour? 'All those things, perhaps,' she thought.

Rashie Coat slipped in at the back of the Kirk and joined in the hymns and prayers. During the service the laird's son, looking about the congregation, set eyes upon her and all through the remaining service kept looking in her direction. Just before the end she slipped out the door, removed the coat and made her way home. At the house, the table was already set and dinner was prepared and ready to serve. There was no sign of the visitor.

The following Sunday, as Rashie Coat once more prepared to cook dinner, her benefactor appeared. 'It is time for you to go to church, young Rashie Coat. Put on your coat of feathers and fly away this instant. I will make sure that all is well here.'

Once again Rashie Coat opened her wicker basket, but this time she took out the coat of feathers and wrapped it about her; again she transformed. Stopping at the door, she recited her little rhyme:

Ae peat gar anither peat burn,
Ae spit gar anither spit turn,
Ae pat gar anither pat play,
Let Rashie Coat gang tae the kirk the day.

As she walked along the High Street she chastised herself for once more not asking the visitor who she was. She slipped into the kirk and joined in the service, loving the joyful singing of the psalms and hymns and struggling not to have her mind wander during the long sermon. The fact that the laird's son could not seem to keep his eyes off her was a distraction, though a little unsettling. Taking advantage of a boisterous rendition of the 23rd Psalm she took her leave and went home. Dinner was ready.

That week rumour abounded in the household that the laird's son was beside himself with love of a strange girl about his own age, who appeared out of nowhere and had disappeared without a trace, only to reappear and disappear again. He had spent the past few days searching for this enigma, without success. Rashie Coat was aware of the talk but made no comment so as not to draw attention to herself. She was secure in the belief that her dowdy and often grimy appearance disguised her true self.

On the following Sunday her angel appeared again. 'It is time for you to go to church, my little princess, and this time you must wear your coat and shoes of rushes.' As she left the house Rashie Coat repeated her rhyme:

Ae peat gar anither peat burn,
Ae spit gar anither spit turn,
Ae pat gar anither pat play,
Let Rashie Coat gang tae the kirk the day.

Before leaving, she looked at the figure before her, at the face that shone with a heavenly light and at the simple yet delicate diadem that adorned her head. There was something so familiar about the presence, but more than that it was the feeling of pure love that emanated from her. Although she loathed leaving, Rashie Coat closed the door and went to the kirk. She lost herself in the crowd and kept a wary lookout for the laird's son. It wasn't long before she became aware of being looked at. The lad had obviously placed himself near the door in anticipation of her arrival. In a restrained panic she quickly made for the door and leaped down the steps. She landed awkwardly and her left shoe came off. As she went back to retrieve it the young man came through the door.

Rashie Coat turned and ran off up the street. She glanced briefly over her shoulder in time to see him pick up the shoe.

The following day, word went out round Dumfries that the laird's son was looking for the young woman who had lost her shoe outside of Greyfriar's Church. As the shoe had obviously been specially made, he would marry the person whose foot it fitted. A queue formed outside the house and girl after girl tried and failed. Gradually the word spread and people came from as far away as Kirkcudbright and Moniaive. The queue grew and grew but the search was fruitless until a mother and her red-headed daughter came all the way from Langholm. When finally the girl had her turn the shoe fitted perfectly, though it was noted that the foot looked, as one maid said, a bit 'nippit an clippit'. And indeed it was, for the hen-wife, remembering that the barefooted Rashie Coat had stepped in mud at her front door, had performed acts of minor mutilation to her daughter's feet to make them the same size as the footprint; so certain was she, by the descriptions given, that it was Rashie Coat the laird's son had sought. The hen-wife decided that the laird's daughter was either dead or over the border and so chanced her luck. It was in. The shoe fitted and the wedding was arranged. So as to end speculation, the laird's son took his bride-to-be on a ride around the town wearing the shoe made of rushes. A little perplexed, but at the same time delighted at finding his lost love, he rode proudly out, she sitting behind him on his great charger. As he rode past Lincluden, a bird in a hawthorn tree sang out:

Nippit fit *and clippit* fit	foot
Ahint *the laird's son rides;*	behind
Whilst bonny fit and pretty fit	
Ahint the caudron *hides.*	cauldron

The little doubt that had niggled at him was fully realised and he tipped the hen-wife's daughter from his horse, leaped off and retrieved the shoe. He rode at once for home and made his way into the scullery; staff quickly stood aside as he entered. Rashie Coat, on hearing the disturbance and loud voices, ducked down behind the water cauldron. The lad knew exactly where to go.

He leaned over the container and proffered a hand to Rashie Coat. She modestly raised her arm and allowed herself to be guided from her hiding place. He undid her mutch and let her hair fall about her shoulders, then he tenderly wiped the ash from her face. As he looked into her eyes, she knew she had, at last, found her one true love. Trying on the shoe was a formality. The fit was perfect, as was the moment. He turned and with a brief nod of his head shooed everyone from the kitchen. Taking her hands in his he leaned forward and very gently and sweetly kissed her. 'Will you marry me?' he asked.

She laughed and threw her arms about him, 'Yes, yes, yes!'

And so in time Ella became the first lady of Dumfries and of Langholm. Although the laird's wife, she treated everyone, regardless of their station, with care and respect and was loved for it. And though she was usually addressed as Mistress or Milady, she was always affectionately known as Rashie Coat. She had great comfort in a loving husband and, eventually, loving children. But what comforted her most was the thought that just out of sight was someone who watched over her.

2

THE MILK-WHITE DOO

Jacob and Wilhelm Grimm collected märchen or folk tales in their native Germany. Their collection is certainly the best known in the world of folk tales. When translated into English, what became apparent to other collectors such as James Halliwell, J.F. Campbell, William Chambers and others was the commonality of many of the tales. No doubt storytellers took tales from books, such as Grimms', that they then used, but more usually the tales were oral and travelled along the highways and seaways of the world every which way: Cinderella probably started in China, hence the shoe only fitting one specific foot, and versions of the famed Brer Rabbit can be found in Africa and China. The following tale would seem to have a common source with the Grimms' 'Juniper Tree', because of the close similarity of the repetitive refrain. But, as in most tales, it takes on something of the culture where it is told. Similar versions are found in Hungary, Romania, Austria and England, and this one is from Scotland. Be warned, it is a shocking tale for adults. Unsurprisingly – to storytellers – it is very popular with children.

Long ago there was a man called Alan Hunter who fell in love with a girl called Belle. Though not the brightest of souls, Alan was loving and kind and relentlessly courted Belle for a year and a day. In the end, she agreed to marry him. The marriage was blissful and they worked together on their little croft on the long plain, *Am Magh Fada* in Gaelic, which gives the town of Moffat its name. Because of their hard work they prospered and so leased more land until they had a substantial farm and moorland for summer grazing. They had a small herd of sheep, six milk cows and numerous chickens, ducks and geese. They also had ten acres of arable land which they formed into rigs, or ridges – unfenced raised strips of soil, for growing oats, barley, hay and flax for clothing. On the in-by fields near the farm they built dykes to safeguard the animals and to keep them away from their crops in the out-by fields.

They had been five years married when winter came early. The land was dusted with snow, yet there were still leaves on the rowan tree that stood to the side, or cheek, of their front door. The young woman looked at the tree and made a wish that she would have a child with hair red like the rowan and skin as fair as the new snow. Soon after, the young woman found she was pregnant, and on a warm day in August she gave birth to a baby boy whom she named Johnnie. He had a shock of thick red hair and his skin seemed to shine white with an inner light. However, the birth was difficult, complications arose and, with no skilled surgeon within fifty miles, she died. Family gathered round and gave Alan support in his grief and a wet nurse was found for the child. In time, Alan settled down to life as a single parent. To remind him of the purity and beauty of his wife, he set two large white quartz stones beneath the rowan tree.

Running the farm on his own was hard and he thought it best and practical to get some extra help. He hired a young, unemployed man called Hugh Bowman who brought along his sister Morag to help in the house. The girl's common-law husband had deserted her, and with a young daughter to care for was glad of the work. While Hugh was an adequate worker, his sister, also not the brightest of souls, was excellent. Morag had a hard edge, and when it came to chopping a chicken for the pot or taking a knife to the throat of a braxy sheep at the back end of the year, she did so without a second thought. What Alan especially liked was that her daughter Katie had great maternal instincts and spent her time playing with Johnnie, who had just started to crawl. She insisted on feeding, washing and generally caring for the boy.

A month later, Hugh was offered a job at a neighbouring farm with a higher wage. Though sad to see him go, Alan was quite happy he did not have to pay out two wages and his own; he could manage with Morag's help. Shortly after, it seemed right and decent to Alan that, if Morag was living under the same roof, perhaps they should be properly married. Morag seemed happy enough with the arrangement, no doubt feeling more secure about Katie's and her future. By this time, Alan loved Katie as if she were his own daughter and was fond of Morag, even with her occasional highly strung emotions. They had a penny wedding where neighbours and friends contributed a penny each to the celebrations. They settled down to family life, and though Morag was occasionally hard on Johnnie, this was mitigated by the obvious affection Katie had for the lad. She also insisted that he should not be called her 'step-brother' but simply her 'brother'.

In the first year of their marriage things went well in the home and on the farm. There was a good harvest and the children especially enjoyed the trip to the mill in Moffat to grind the corn. They paid the miller in meal then took a bag – the melder – to poor people in the village. Alan also visited the local silversmith and had a bracelet made for Morag – he missed the look of disappointment in Katie's eyes as they passed the dress shop that she had not got something, though he did buy liquorice to make sugarallie water:

Sugarallie *water,*	lichorice
as black as the lum,	chimney
If ye gether up yer preens,	pins
I'll gie *ye some.*	give

they sang as they poured hot water over the black sticks.

The second year of their marriage was hard. It had been especially rainy and the crops had not thrived. The animals suffered in the wet pasture and grew less healthy, and some died. Milk production dropped and Alan was loathed to shear the sheep in the continuing cold. Taking the sheep on to the hill was misery but he had to herd them against theft. His oilskins kept out the worst of the rain but he could never sit for any length of time as he would grow cold. While his dogs never complained, they looked quite miserable. Back on the farm, the children kept a watchful eye on the cattle when they were out-by to stop them straying into the meagre crops. Morag kept house, did spinning and sowing and looking after the poultry, though even their egg production had dwindled; only the ducks and geese seemed impervious to the wet. Although not on the point of starvation, other people were, and things were worrying, for animals were disappearing from neighbouring farms. Alan decided that he would take his musket with him next time he took the sheep to the hill. For a change, the evening was dry and pleasant and the sun setting to the north-north-west sank into a bed of fire. The night would be light, but it was time he was home to see the children before bed. He had only gone twenty yards when a hare rose in front of him. On impulse, he raised the musket and fired. It was a clean shot and the animal dropped instantly. At the same time the sheep fled the bang, as did the sheepdogs. It was late before he had gathered them up and herded them back to the farm. Morag was piqued at the late arrival and the children were already asleep. He dropped the hare on the table and explained what had occurred. She replied, 'Huv ye nae brain? Ye micht hae kennt the blast wid send them fleein.'

Because of tiredness and having been teased mercilessly about his brawn and no brain as a child, Alan fumed, 'Caain the kettle black? Ye hae little wit yersel!'

With the stress of present circumstances, both exploded into fury and railed at each other, waking the children in the process. The howls and tears of the children quietened the feuding pair. That night Alan slept on the rug by the fire. First thing in the morning he was away to the hill with the sheep.

When Morag rose from her sleep, darkness had crept into her soul; deep resentments murmured along the boundaries of her mind; confusion and madness skirmished in her thoughts. As if in a trance, she saw to the children's breakfast then sent them to let out the poultry and collect any eggs while she milked the cows, slapping at them furiously if they moved. While the children took the cows to the out-by pasture, Morag strained the milk, put in the churn then went back into the house to prepare the hare. With manic relish she gutted and skinned the carcase and placed it in the cauldron. Wielding the kitchen knife like a weapon of war she chopped onions, carrots and parsnips, dropped them into the pot and added some water. She set it to hang just above the fire to slow-cook. After an hour she added more peats and stirred the stew. Two hours later, as she added more peats, she couldn't resist a taste of the flesh. It was delicious. She found herself returning again and again to the stew until there were only vegetables left. Maniacally she paced the room, knife in hand, muttering threats and fears about Alan: 'I should poison the damned stew. But he'll go for me again; might even beat me if there's no hare in the pot.' Just then, Johnnie toddled through the door; his innocent face looked up at his step-mother. In that moment Morag's mind snapped. She lifted Johnnie by the arm, placed him on the table and chopped his head off. She dismembered the body, dropped it all into the cauldron and brought it to the boil with some brushwood. The stew was then gently simmered for the rest of the day. As it cooked, Morag threw herself down on the bed and fell asleep.

Katie, who was sitting on a rock looking after the cows, watched Johnnie as he padded off towards the farm. As he went round a building out of sight she kept an eye out for his return. He was gone too long so she decided to run back to the farm to get him – the cows were hobbled so it was safe to leave them for five minutes. She first checked the outbuildings then, not finding him, went to the house. The door was open and she could see her mother asleep on the bed. She looked in the door but could not see Johnnie. The sweet smell of cooking was overpowering so she went over to the cauldron and peeped in. Looking back at her was the face of her brother. She reeled back gasping in horror. The sound woke Morag who sat up and rubbed her eyes. Katie looked at her mother with shock and fear. Morag rose from the bed with a look of fury. She took two steps across the floor and grabbed Katie by the hair. She leaned forward to within a few inches of Katie's face, 'If ye say a word o this tae yer faither ye will end up in the pot yersel. Dae ye unnerstaun?' Her face white with terror and her eyes brimming with tears of fear and loss, Katie could barely nod. Her mother threw her to the floor, 'Get oot o ma sicht an see tae they coos.' The lass ran from the house towards the meadow, howling in distress. She had watched her mother over the years and could never understand why sometimes she would seem caring then other times she would become like a demon, though rarely in front of Alan. It was the children who suffered most.

Katie stayed away all day, too much in terror of what might happen when she returned. She delayed as late as possible until the cows became agitated and began hobbling towards the farm. She undid the hobbles and the cows sprinted off towards the byre. They arrived at the same time as Alan and the sheep from the hill, which were driven in beside the cows for security. Katie arrived just as Alan was chaining and padlocking the door. He stepped forward, put his hands under her armpits, lifted her and planted a kiss on her cheeks. 'Hoo are ye, ma bonnie wee lass?' Although she felt safer now he was home, she dreaded what was to come and could not look him in the face. Instead she laid her head on his shoulder and snuggled in. She felt his powerful hand gently stroke her hair as they went in the house.

Although the atmosphere inside was tense, Alan, while setting Katie down, attempted to ease things, 'My, that's a grand smell. What is it?' he said amiably.

'It's the hare that ye shot,' Morag said abruptly, throwing a threatening look at Katie.

'Disnae smell like hare,' he replied innocently.

'That's because I pit ither things in the pot as weel,' she said sarcastically.

'Aye, of course.'

Alan went to the sideboard and carried over four wooden bowls and four horn spoons.

'Jist set it fer twa,' said Morag, 'I'm no hungry and the boy's sleepin.'

Alan set two places and put two bowls and spoons back on the sideboard.

'I'm no hungersome either,' said Katie, before sloping off to bed in tears.

'Whit's up wi the weans?' asked Alan.

'Nae idea,' said Morag, Picking up Alan's bowl and walking over to the cauldron. She ladled the stew into the bowl and set it before Alan. He supped a spoonful of juice before lifting some onion.

Through the curtain of the inset bed, Katie looked on in horror as she saw him lift a spoonful of flesh. It slipped off the spoon and fell back in the bowl. Katie willed him not to pick it up again. Instead of using his spoon, he picked it up with his fingers.

'Would ye luik at that,' he said, with a laugh. 'It luiks jist like wee Johnnie's haun.'

Katie gasped and threw herself face down on the heather-flower pillow.

'Yer haiverin,' said Morag. 'It wis a muckle hare.'

Alan ate the limb and set about the rest with relish. Halfway through he picked up another piece of flesh, gave a laugh and said, 'That's like wee Johnnie's fit.'

Katie pressed the pillow into her ears so as not to hear any more.

'Wid ye haud yer wheesht an jist eat yer meat,' said Morag sharply.

Alan made a face of resignation and finished his meal. After he had finished, Morag blew out the candles. 'Bedtime,' she said, expecting no protest.

Katie lay awake and heard her mother and father fall asleep. There was still some light in the sky from the summer sun and a full moon. With the silence of a cat, she climbed from the bed and made her way to the cauldron. She eased it off the pot hook and carried it to the door. As she lifted the sneck, the click caused Alan to stir. Katie stood in silence until he had settled then slid open the door and stepped outside, pulling the door towards her without closing it. She went to the toolstore to get a bucket. With the bucket in one hand and the cauldron in the other, she walked down to the burn. There under the light of a ghost moon she quietly and reverently removed Johnnie's bones from the cauldron, washed each one in the clear water and placed them in the bucket.

Katie then walked back to the door of the house, set down the cauldron and bucket and lifted the quartz stones. Using a flat stone, she dug out the soil and then placed Johnnie's bones in the hole. Next she covered them with the quartz. Using the flat stone she scattered the spare soil from the hole, careful to tread it flat with her feet. After replacing the bucket in the toolstore she went back to the quartz stone, kneeled down and kissed it. She then kissed the rowan tree, gathered up the cauldron and crept back into the house. The cauldron went back on the hook and then Katie slipped into bed. She lay for ages thinking about her beloved brother and his gruesome fate as hot tears dripped on to the pillow; gradually sleep overtook her.

As dawn paled the eastern sky the rowan began to quiver and a small shower of leaves floated down on to the quartz. As for the bones that lay beneath:

They grew, and they grew,
Tae a milk-white doo,   dove
That tuik tae *its wings,*   took to
An awa *it flew.*   away

The bird flew off in the direction of Moffat. When it came to the
River Annan it turned north until it came to a group of women
gossiping at the shallows as they washed new garments to make
ready to sell. The dove alighted on an alder tree and began to coo:

Pew, pew, ma mammy me slew,
Pew, pew, ma daddy me chew,
Ma dear sister Katie she getherit ma banes,   gathered my bones
An set them ablow *twa milk-white stanes;*   below
Whaur I grew, and grew tae a milk-white doo,
Then I tuik to my wings, and awa I flew.

Fascinated by the dove's refrain, one cried out:

Wee doo, wee doo, oh bonnie wee doo
Wid ye sing yer wee sang again fer us noo?

The dove cocked its head to side and said:

Aye, if ye wull cease yer clashin   gossip
An gie me aa the claes ye're washin.

They all looked at each other and nodded, so the dove repeated
the refrain,

Pew, pew, ma mammy me slew,
Pew, pew, ma daddy me chew,
Ma dear sister Katie she getherit ma banes,
An set them ablow twa milk-white stanes;
Whaur I grew, and grew tae a milk-white doo,
Then I tuik to my wings, and awa I flew.

The women laid aside the garments and the dove flew down and, with unearthly strength, lifted the clothes in its claws and flew on towards Moffat. It set the clothes down on a roof and flew on to the window ledge of the silversmith. The smith was just sitting down at his workbench and had laid out a pile of silver coins that he was about to melt down and turn into jewellery when the dove began to call:

Pew, pew, ma mammy me slew,
Pew, pew, ma daddy me chew,
Ma dear sister Katie she getherit ma banes,
An set them ablow twa milk-white stanes;
Whaur I grew, and grew tae a milk-white doo,
Then I tuik to my wings, and awa I flew.

The jeweller turned and stared in fascination at the bird on his window sill.

My, whit an antrin *sang ye sing.*   strange
Wull ye sing it again, ma bonnie wee thing?

Hopping on to the window frame, the dove said:

I wull sing the sang fer ye
If aa yer siller *coins ye'll gie.*   silver

The smith nodded his head and laid the coins on the window sill, and the milk-white dove sang his song:

Pew, pew, ma mammy me slew,
Pew, pew, ma daddy me chew,
Ma dear sister Katie she getherit ma banes,
An set them ablow twa milk-white stanes;
Whaur I grew, and grew tae a milk-white doo,
Then I tuik to my wings, and awa I flew.

With claws and beak he gathered up the coins and flew on to the roof. Wrapping the coins in the clothes he flew to the mill. Leaving the clothes and coins on the roof, the dove flew down and through the mill door. The miller had opened the millrace and set the millwheel turning. He engaged the grinding stones and turned to get a bag of meal sitting against a spare millstone. The dove settled on a beam above the miller's head and began to call out:

Pew, pew, ma mammy me slew,
Pew, pew, ma daddy me chew,
Ma dear sister Katie she getherit ma banes,
An set them ablow twa milk-white stanes;
Whaur I grew, and grew tae a milk-white doo,
Then I tuik to my wings, and awa I flew.

Even over the sound of the turning stones, the plaintive call could be clearly heard. The miller disconnected the gear and turned to the dove:

Hoch! Hoch! Ma bonnie wee doo
Will ye sing for me again een nou?   even (right) now

The bird fluttered down on to the spare millstone:

I will sing ma sang again
If ye will gie me this mill stane.

The miller nodded his head, agreeing to the bargain.

Pew, pew, ma mammy me slew,
Pew, pew, ma daddy me chew,
Ma dear sister Katie she getherit ma banes,
An set them ablow twa milk-white stanes;
Whaur I grew, and grew tae a milk-white doo,
Then I tuik to my wings, and awa I flew.

The dove now grabbed the great millstone in its claws and, to the astonishment of the miller, lifted it into the air and flew out through the open door. Hovering in the air beside the roof, the dove took up the clothes and coins in its beak and flew southwards back towards the farm. Further down the river was an old dead tree. The dove hovered by it, leaning the great stone against its trunk. The clothes with the coins it hung among the dried-out branches, then perched on a twig and waited.

As the sun set it flew on to the farm, gliding in after Alan had come home. It gently laid the millstone against the back of the house and dropped the clothes and coins on the thatch of the roof. It then flew to the ground and gathered up small stones in its beak; these it dropped down the chimney.

Inside Katie lay on the bed in a state of misery. She heard the sound from the fireplace as the pebbles fell into or bounced off the cauldron. Somehow she knew it was a message and ran for the door. Outside, she automatically looked up to see beautiful new clothes floating down towards her. With joy she reached up and caught them.

In the same instant Alan came through the door, curious at Katie's behaviour, in time to see Katie reach up for the falling garments. He looked up to see where they had come from and as he did so ten silver coins flashed past his head and bounced on the ground at his feet. With a laugh, he picked them up then looked again to the sky but nothing was there. In puzzlement, he looked at Katie's smiling face.

On seeing her daughter's strange behaviour and hearing Alan's laugh, Morag walked out the door to see what was happening. Outside, both Katie and Alan were looking in amazement towards the sky. She looked up but only had a brief moment to see the great mass of the millstone falling towards her. The impact was so great that the monolith sank right up to its rim in the ground.

So fast had things happened that Alan and Katie had not seen Morag emerge from the house and so, caught up in the sight of the dove as it hovered like an angel above them, they did not see the fatal act. It was the sound of the impact that turned their heads in shock. They looked up again to the dove as it hovered in the soft blue light of the evening sky. With a soft coo it began to ascend higher and higher. They followed its now glittering whiteness as it soared upwards until it disappeared into the heavens.

Through sobs, Katie told all that had happened the day before. Alan was stricken with guilt and horrified at the idea that he had eaten the flesh of his own son; but Katie said that the dove was the departing spirit of Johnnie and the coins were proof that he must not feel such things. She proved the point by lifting the quartz stones; there was nothing beneath them except three milk-white feathers.

Alan raised Katie as his own, and in time she married an honest young man from Moffat. A year later they had a son and named him Johnnie.

The Croodin Doo

'Whaur hae ye been aa the day,
Ma bonny wee croodin doo?'   cooing dove
'O I hae been at my stepmither's hoose;
Mak ma bed, mammie, noo!
Mak ma bed, mammie, noo!'

'Whaur did ye get yer denner,   dinner
Ma bonny wee croodin doo?'
'I got it in ma stepmither's;
Mak ma bed, mammie, noo, noo noo!
Mak ma bed, mammie, noo!'

'Whit did she gie ye, tae yer denner,
Ma bonny wee croodin doo?'
'She gied me a wee fower-fittit fish;   gave, four footed
Mak my bed, mammie, noo, noo, noo!
Make my bed, mammie, noo!'

'Whaur got she the fower-fittit fish,
Ma bonny wee croodin doo?'
'She got it doon in yon well strand;   yonder
O mak ma bed, mammie, noo, noo, noo!
Mak ma bed mammie noo!'

'Whit did she dae wi the banes o't,   of it
Ma bonny wee croodin doo?'
'She gied them tae the wee dug;   dog
Mak ma bed, mammie, noo, noo, noo!
Mak ma bed, mammie, noo!'

'O whit became o the wee dug,
Ma bonny wee croodin doo?'
'O it shot oot its feet an deeit!   died
O mak ma bed, mammie, noo, noo, no!
O mak my bed, mammie, noo!'

ELPHIN IRVING

The Faery Queen's Cupbearer

Long ago, after the Frost Giants and the Lord of the Wind had retreated to their fortress of the north, grass, flowers and forests returned with the wolf and the deer, and with them, humankind. The immortal elves that had borne the long winter in their homes in the hollow hills appeared. They danced on the hillsides and revelled in the glens; they sang, spreading joy among mortal folk. They prepared flavoursome feasts whose fare softened even the most hardened Presbyterian heart. Their music flowed into the human soul and filled it with strange and glamorous longing and a deep beautiful melancholy. Even in the latter days, when man's religion had degraded them as the sons and daughters of evil, they were secretly loved by the common folk as the 'guid neichbours' or the 'guid folk'. In time, man's sickle and axe drove them west until their last refuge in the Borderlands was in the upland glen of Corriewater that lies between Eskdalemuir and Lockerbie. From here they made their 'Faery Rade', when all the denizens of Elfland would ride out behind the Faery King and Queen. Those so bold as to witness the procession would often see, among the ranks, a cousin lost in battle, a friend who had sailed on a doomed ship, perhaps even a stolen child. Those with extraordinary courage might then, through enormous trial, deliver them back to the human world.

In these long ago times, on the banks of Corriewater, there stood a shepherd's cottage, made of drystone and thatched with heather and bracken. On the cottage walls grew sweet-scented honeysuckle and columbine. About the building were a well-stocked kailyard and an orchard of plum, cherry and apple. Nearby, under the roots of a sessile oak, was a spring from which flowed clear, sweet water. The shepherd and his wife who lived there had a boy and girl: twins entirely devoted to each other. Elphin and Phemie Irving spent their days playing by Corrie or helping their parents with cooking or tending the sheep. Phemie had a particular aptitude for shepherding and was happiest out on the moor helping tend her father's flock. In their sixteenth year, their father, while attempting to drag a waterlogged sheep from a sudden spate on the river, was himself dragged under the fast-flowing stream and drowned. Three days later, when he was buried, their mother took herself to her bed and within a week joined her husband in his grave.

The twin's inheritance was seventeen acres of arable pasture, seven milk cows, seven pot sheep, seven bonnet-pieces of gold and a broadsword and spear an ancestor had wielded at the Battle of Dryfe Sands between Lochmaben and Lockerbie in 1593. Though young, both were wise in the ways of survival and thrived. As both grew, their haunting good looks attracted the attention of the young people of the area. At fairs, ceilidhs and weddings young men were in competition to dance with Phemie; a smile, a look or especially a touch of her hand sent them into raptures. Many a young heart praised her in song and rhyme. Even the young women were moved to composition, praising the shining brow of Elphin. However, Phemie would only pay attention to the friends of Elphin and always at a distance. When these friends departed for a twilight tryst Elphin and Phemie would return home and continue their chores. His duty was always to Phemie and hers to him: they were at their happiest in each other's company.

While Elphin ploughed their land or planted, Phemie tended the animals, milking the cows or herding the sheep on the hillside. Where she wandered, the wild animals were unafraid and deer would graze happily as she passed. Even the birds seemed at ease in her company. Thus it was until their nineteenth year when there was little to no rain from April until August, Their pasture was a brown desert; even the river was no more than a trickle. People moved their cattle on to the high ground and into the depleted lochs and drying bogs where there were still green plants to eat. Times were lean and hard, so Elphin took over the task of tending Phemie's sheep as well as the cattle for fear of theft. Phemie stayed at home looking after the house and keeping an eye on their new brood of hens. At evening, Elphin would bring in the beasts from the hill and take them further up the river to drink from the shrinking pools and to graze the few green grasses and plants that still clung to the bank.

On a late August evening Phemie was standing by the cottage door watching the skyline for a sight of her brother. The day had been hot and a violent storm had raged across the moors some miles away. The sun had now set and the first stars were glittering above. Nearby, the usual faint sound of trickling water was replaced by a more urgent sound as storm water from the high moor found its way into the glen. She was concerned, for Elphin was usually home by sunset. As she peered up the darkening glen the water appeared to shimmer and brighten, then a wild light danced over the stream, flashing from bank to bank. The chaos of illuminations transformed into human shape and glided from the river into the house. So like her brother in form and grace was the figure that she ran into the house expecting to see him. The house was empty; the vision or wraith was gone. In that instant she lost all composure and, in a fit of terror, screamed herself senseless.

Late the following morning a young female friend from a neighbouring croft dropped by and found Phemie sitting in her chair. He skin had transformed to marble white and her usually immaculate hair now hung in disorder about her neck and shoulders. Her gaze was firmly fixed on her brother's chair. The young lass greeted Phemie but she gave no response. 'Dinnae be sae disheartened aboot yer loss, Phemie. Seven o yer sheep are saved and we can gie ye a pickle mair. Naebody expectit Corriewater tae gang in spate sae sudden. It was leapin frae bank tae bank in nae

time.' Phemie was unmoved and, seemingly unaware of her friend, continued to stare at the chair.

'If ye juist send Elphin ower tae us he can help tae herd the yowes back here.'

At the mention of her brother's name Phemie seemed to come alive and wildly declared, 'Whaur is he? Whaur is he?' before dropping senseless to the floor. People from around Corrievale, concerned by the flooding and seeing sheep and hay floating down the river, came to offer assistance and helped to care for Phemie until she revived. For Phemie, consciousness was a worse state, filled with unbearable pain and sorrow. 'They hae taen him, they hae taen him; he that was fairer than the lily on Lyddal Lee. Lang did they seek him, and in the end een my prayers cuidnae save him. They came wi sang and charm and their unbaptised hauns hae glamourised his baptised brou. He was too bonnie, too guid and too noble for the sons and dochters o man. Fer whit are we compared to him: muinlicht tae the sun, a caunle tae the evenin sterne. I saw them comin fer him, they dauncit and sang as they placed him upon a horse that was neer shod wi iron. They bore him awa ower water and hill. But I will find him fer I hae heard their wondrous music i the wild wid. This baptised child will be his deliverance.' Phemie looked about her into a sea of sympathetic tear-stained faces, 'Ye dinnae believe me. Ye think he is deid, deep droont in Corrie Water. Search, search as ye micht, aye and ye micht find a body tae wrap in a windin sheet and drap yer tears upon i the graveyaird. But I tell ye, he is in the service o Elfland and I will release him. Nou gang aboot yer business. I hae my hair tae knot and my hoose tae prepare.'

The people of Corrievale, upset at the loss of Elphin Irving and alarmed at Phemie's state of mind, continued to search along the stream now that the water had, in the main, subsided. Six sheep from the flock were found but because the water was still peaty brown nothing was visible under shelves and tree roots. Even when the water fully subsided and cleared, no sign of Elphin was to be found. 'He wis o the faery himsel,' some said, 'a changelin, drappet intae a Christian cradle. Nou they hae taen him back.' Faery or not, many a maiden would have been glad of a tryst with him. 'His manner, his voice, hou he daunced, an thae merry, blue een; he cuid glamour me onytime.'

Some of those of a more superstitious nature who had heard the delirious speech of Phemie were convinced of his abduction and chose not to meet with their lovers in the evening for fear that they might too join the ranks of Elfland. Some said they had seen the 'Faery Rade', others knew of abducted children that the faery folk had used to pay Satan his due. Someone paid mention to the fact that Elphin's and Phemie's mother had a cousin who was burned as a witch. And so the lore grew and took on a life of its own.

Some days later another storm raged across the hills bringing down greater torrents of water into the glen. Through the early morning storm rode a farmer, the Laird of Johnstonebank, who had been across at a Borders' fair and had travelled back overnight. He rode a fine strong garron and was well clothed in a cloak of plaid beneath which he wore a greatcoat; both were soaked in natural lanolin and quite waterproof. As he entered the remains of the great Caledonian forest that lined the banks of Corriewater his horse shied and drew back. Supernatural fear struck the farmer; all the more intensified by recent local rumours. Fearing he might be attacked by a bogle, or worse, he urged the horse forward with a quick dig of his spurs. It continued to start from side to side, pricking its ears towards trees and bushes. The farmer's unease increased as the path rose up towards a knoll from which rose a giant oak tree. The knoll formed what was locally known as a fairy ring. The farmer started in shock because among the great tree's roots sat a young woman. She was dressed in white from neck to

knee, her arms and lower limbs naked and her hair hung loose in a
chaos of curls. Her arms constantly moved, throwing back her hair,
her gaze on the road that wound down to an ancient graveyard.
Suddenly she seemed electrified and leaped to her feet and began
to dance round the oak chanting:

The Fairy Oak of Corriewater

The small bird's head is under its wing,
The deer sleeps on the grass;
The moon comes out, and the stars shine down,
The dew gleams like the glass:
There is no sound in the world so wide,
Save the sound of the smitten brass,
With the merry cittern and the pipe
Of the fairies as they pass.
But oh! the fire maun *burn and burn,*   may
And the hour is gone, and will never return.

The green hill cleaves, and forth, with a bound,
 Comes elf and elfin steed;
The moon dives down in a golden cloud,
The stars grow dim with dread;
But a light is running along the earth,
So of heaven's they have no need:
O'er moor and moss with a shout they pass,
And the word is spur and speed–
But the fire maun burn, and I maun quake,
And the hour is gone that will never come back.

And when they came to Craigyburnwood,
The Queen of the Fairies spoke:
'Come, bind your steeds to the rushes so green,
And dance by the haunted oak:
I found the acorn on Heshbon Hill,

In the nook of a palmer's poke,
A thousand years since; here it grows!'
And they danced till the greenwood shook:
But oh! the fire, the burning fire,
The longer it burns, it but blazes the higher.

'I have won me a youth,' the Elf Queen said,
'The fairest that earth may see;
This night I have won young Elph Irving
My cupbearer to be.
His service lasts but for seven sweet years,
And his wage is a kiss of me.'
And merrily, merrily, laughed the wild elves
Round Corrie's greenwood tree.
But oh! the fire it glows in my brain,
And the hour is gone, and comes not again.

The Queen she has whispered a secret word,
'Come hither, my Elphin sweet,
And bring that cup of the charmèd wine,
Thy lips and mine to meet.'
But a brown elf shouted a loud, loud shout,
'Come, leap on your coursers fleet,
For here comes the smell of some baptised flesh
And the sound of baptised feet.'
But oh! the fire that burns, and maun burn;
For the time that is gone will never return.

On a steed as white as the new-milked milk,
The Elf Queen leaped with a bound,
And young Elphin a steed like December snow
'Neath him at the word he found.
But a maiden came, and her christened arms
She linked her brother around,
And called on God, and the steed with a snort

Sank into the gaping ground.
But the fire maun burn, and I maun quake,
And the time that is gone will no more come back.

And she held her brother, and lo! he grow
A wild bull waked in ire;
And she held her brother, and lo! he changed
To a river roaring higher;
And she held her brother, and he became
A flood of the raging fire;
She shrieked and sank, and the wild elves laughed
Till the mountain rang and mire.
But oh! the fire yet burns in my brain,
And the hour is gone, and comes not again.

'O maiden, why waxed thy faith so faint,
Thy spirit so slack and slaw?
Thy courage kept good till the flame waxed wud,
Then thy might began to thaw;
Had ye kissed him with thy christened lip,
Ye had wan him frae "mang us a".
Now bless the fire, the elfin fire,
That made thee faint and fa';
Now bless the fire, the elfin fire,
The longer it burns it blazes the higher.'

The farmer sat mesmerised and enchanted by this strange creature dancing in the growing light of dawn. At first he thought it some angelic vision, then, realising it was Phemie Irving, he urged the horse forward. She at once let out a scream of joy and rushed to him, throwing her arms about his waist, 'I hae ye nou Elphin, I hae ye nou.'

'What ails ye lass?' said Johnstonebank kindly. Phemie looked up into his eyes, gasped and fainted.

The farmer dismounted, lifted Phemie's fragile form and carried her down into the glen. At the same time two shepherds came

along the riverbank carrying the lifeless body of Elphin Irving. They had found the body turning in an eddy, his hands clutching clumps of wool. Like his father, he had drowned trying to save their sheep. The laird removed his plaidie and wrapped it about Elphin. They carried Phemie and her brother to a nearby cottage. While the guidwife cared for Phemie, Elphin's body was taken into a small side chamber and laid on a paliasse. The laird removed the plaidie from off of the boy's body and he, the husband and shepherds then discussed the probable circumstances of the death. The door suddenly burst open and Phemie entered, laughing wildly. She looked down at Elphin's waxen face, 'Wunnerfu, sae wunnerfu. This thing wrocht by the faery folk tae fool ye into believin it is ma brither; but it is no. Ye socht the leevin saul and fand anely the garment; fer I saw him this past nicht riding oot wi the ranks o Elfland, he by far the fairest. Hud ye but grespit him an held ticht whilst he shapeshiftit throu aa the terrifyin guises an forms o the itherwarld. Hud ye grippit on, tho yer flesh burnit and yer hert froze, then ye wuid hae beheld the true Elphin Irving.'

'But hearken! Hearken! On Hallowmass Eve, when the denizens o the yirth are set free an King and Queen of Elfland ride oot, then I will mak ma staund at Corrie's burial grund. When Elphin an his troop pass I will loup on him an win him, or perish.' This said, she fell, tears streaming, upon the lifeless form, 'Ma brither! Oh, ma brither!' She was carried insensible from the room.

Phemie recovered then relapsed into her delirium right through the burial of Elphin and up to Hallowmass Eve. That night she disappeared from her cottage. She was found, covered in rime, in the ancient graveyard, her back to a faded gravestone and her intense eyes looking along the old road. Alas, the spirit of the fairest maid in Annandale had fled.

4

THE CARLINS O CAIRNSMORE

Abram Fell was a young man of an honest and decent disposition. To cap it all, he had inherited lands along the fertile banks of the River Tweed, so he set out to claim his right. His joy at his prospects was cut short when it was discovered that there was a missing document from the deeds that proved him to be the rightful heir. The solicitor for the estate informed him that unless the document could be found he would not be able to take possession of the estate.

Unable to even guess where to look, Abram took to the road in despair. He wandered as far as the Pentland Hills brooding at his misfortune. Tired and weary, he threw himself down among the heather and fell into a deep slumber. His sleep was fitful with unchancy images haunting the edge of his dreams. From among them came a voice urging him to make haste to Bonnie Galloway, for there he would find his heart's desire.

Buoyed up with hope, Abram set out on the long road by way of the Dalvine Pass, Thornhill and Moniaive. In time he reached the banks of Dee, stopping a while in Crossmichael, then Kirkcudbright. Being of good nature, fair of face and with a little money, he soon found favour with the young lasses of the district, and all without incurring the jealousy of its young men. In truth, he was interested in no one but the beautiful Katie Bell.

She was lithe, with silken-blond hair, gleaming blue eyes and a laugh that made his heart dance. Fortunately for Abram, Katie felt the same. Unfortunately for the young man, Katie was the only child of the Laird of Burnilee, a rich man who considered no one within a hundred miles worthy of his fair child. When Abram, now somewhat poorer and shabbily dressed, approached him for Katie's hand in marriage, the laird spurned him, 'My daughter has no interest in a vagabond like you except perhaps as a mere distraction,' and drove him from his door, the laird's mocking laughter ringing in his ears. Abram almost ran from the tower, sick and distraught at the laird's words, little knowing that Katie had thrown herself on to her bed, sobbing with grief at her father's rage and the loss of her one true love.

'I came to Galloway to find my heart's desire and all I find is heartache.' Abram escaped to the rivers and streams, chasing the wily salmon in an attempt to keep his mind from his troubles. But all was to no avail, so he snapped his rod in two and fled to the woods and the hills.

Soon after, Katie disappeared. One moment she was in her room, the next moment, gone. A massive search was organised but

not even a footprint was found. As the search spread ever further, blame was heaped on Abram Fell, that somehow he had kidnapped the lass. Suspicion was laid to rest when the Laird of Burnilee's men found Abram wandering alone in the fastness of the mountains. In obvious distress, Abram joined the search, but nothing could be found of his lover. Leaving the laird to his lamentations, Abram took refuge in a mountain bothy, lonely and sad.

What no one knew was that the Daoine Sith, the fairy folk, so upset by Katie's grief, had spirited her away to the depths of their home beneath the great, granite mass of Cairnsmore. They dressed her in the finest silks and satins, placed rings on her fingers and toes, wrapped bangles about her wrists and hung jewels about her neck. They brought the finest sweetmeats and danced graceful cotillions about her, eager to bring her out of her misery. She gave a frail smile in gratitude but promptly fell back into grief and sorrow.

The elves were at a loss and consulted shellycoats, sacbauns, glaistigs and bauchans. However, it was a wise old brownie that had the answer, 'Up on the slopes of Curleywee you will find a half-derelict mountain bothy and therein is a young man by the name of Abram Fell. He is the cause of her grief.'

'How shall we dispose of him?' asked a bauchan.

The brownie raised his eyes to the ceiling. 'We shall not be disposing of him. What I mean is, she is in love with young Mr Fell and it is for him she grieves.' The bauchan gave a look of disappointment.

'I think it best if we send a couple of bogles to bring him to us,' said an elf, 'It's what Her Majesty would wish.' And so it was done.

Before he knew what was happening, Abram was bound and dispatched to Cairnsmore. He was much relieved to find out he was not to be the bogles' supper – not that there was much meat on him anyway. He caught a glimpse of himself in a mirror and was shocked at his appearance: clothes in tatters, his eyes sunk into hollow and pallid cheeks. The elves gave him a draught of golden liquor that repaired him almost instantly. Suitably refreshed, they dressed him in a blue velvet suit, placed a red velvet cap upon his head and topped it with a white owl's feather.

Now that he was presentable, two elves, as tall as himself, led Abram deeper into the mountain. They passed through magnificent rooms clothed in silks and satins and adorned with exquisite furniture. Many were inhabited by strange and wonderful creatures that bowed to him as he passed. In the heart of the mountain he entered a giant hall that glittered and shone with the lights of a thousand candles that appeared to float in the air. The walls were encrusted with jewels that radiated the candlelight until the entire room glowed in splendour. At the far end of the hall was a gilded throne on which sat a woman who outshone all that surrounded her. Adam was escorted into her presence. Without even thinking, he automatically bowed. She nodded and smiled kindly.

'You know who I am, Master Fell?'

Abram looked at the powerful face of the woman before him. Her expression was kindly, but he could see in her eyes a fierce and deadly power, 'Yes Ma'am. You are the Carlin Queen.'

She laughed. 'Yes, that is what the sons of Adam call me. But I am no mere witch queen, nor even a witch. No Abram, I am the Bànrigh na Sìthichean, what you might call the faery queen, though that name is more suited to those who reign in the Saxon lands to the south. Alas, they are being driven out by the scythe and the ploughshare. For the moment we are safe here in the fastness of Galloway: the sons of Adam have not yet devised a scythe or plough that will cut furrows in granite.'

'May they never,' said Abram.

'Indeed,' said the Bànrigh thoughtfully. 'Now, young Abram, what do you think of our mountain home?'

'It is a wondrous place, Your Majesty, and I am humbled to be here and in your presence.'

She smiled. 'Manners worthy of the Daoine Sìth.'

'What is the deena she?'

'Daoine Sìth is the ancient name of the faery folk.'

'Long may they live and long may you reign over them.' Abram bowed.

'We were right to bring you here and here you may stay for as long as you wish.'

'Your Majesty is most gracious, bu—'

The Bànrigh raised a finger to her mouth that cut short Abram's words. 'Before you say more, come with me.'

She stepped down from the throne and moved towards a great door to her right. Abram followed, noticing that she seemed to glide rather than walk. 'You have seen many wonderful things Abram, but now I will show you what will be, to you, the most wondrous of all.'

Along an ornately arched passage they came to a studded oaken door. She lifted her hand and the door swung open soundlessly. Abram was beckoned to enter, 'Your heart's desire is here.'

Abram walked into the room alone, wondering what to expect. Inside was as ornately decorated as all the others but for a large four-poster bed. Lying on it, face buried in the pillows and fast asleep, was a young woman. A puzzled look came on to his face. That was, until he recognised the silken hair. He briefly turned to the Bànrigh, who smiled and departed the room, closing the door behind her. Abram tiptoed across the room and sat on the edge of the bed. Gently he laid a hand on the young woman's head. 'Katie,' he said softly.

The young woman stirred and slowly turned. Her eyes opened then double-blinked before she threw her arms around Abram, 'You came for me.' She hugged him tighter. 'You came for me.'

'I did look for you. But it was the Carlins, I mean, the Good Neighbours, who brought me here.'

'You are here, and that's all that matters.'

They lay for a while in each other's arms, until a knock on the door separated them. Abram walked to the door and opened it. Surrounded by a band of unchancy creatures was the Bànrigh. 'I wish both of you to come with me,' she said. Arm in arm, Abram and Katie followed her Royal Highness all the way to the great hall. As they entered, crowds of faery folk entered from the hall's many doors. The Bànrigh seated herself on her throne then beckoned the couple forward. She then placed sea-ivory bracelets in their wrists. 'Join hands,' she commanded. 'With these tokens of love I join you as man and woman for the rest of your lives. To confirm this, you may kiss each other.'

Abram looked in amazement at the Bànrigh; but before he could turn his head, Katie planted a kiss on the side of his mouth. He laughed in surprise before returning the embrace. A band struck up and around them the Daoine Sìth began to dance a cotillion. Automatically, Abram and Katie joined the throng as it swayed and glided round the great hall. In the joy and beauty of the moment all thoughts of the outside world departed.

Assuming that they were of the Daoine Sìth, Abram and Katie spent their time wandering in their subterranean paradise, lost in the wonder and beauty of it. They found secret rooms, grottoes and deep, dark pools of crystal water to sit by or bathe in. Weeks and months slipped past unnoticed as they wandered this vast underworld. Eventually they found their way to the great library of the Sìth. Here were ancient works written in familiar and strange texts: manuscripts from across the world, and across time. There were bound volumes of vellum with sublime illustrations and illuminated script in bright colours edged with gold. They read magic spells, lost histories and saw exotic birds and animals that were part of storytellers' tales. Abram also found a simple rolled document bound with a silk ribbon. Though quite plain – and because of that – it grabbed his attention. Untying the ribbon he spread it out on a grand mahogany table. Two words leaped off the page at him: Abram Fell. As he scanned the page, he realised it was the very document that proved his inheritance. Providence and a strange dream had led him here. Or was it?

They made their way to the great hall and begged an audience with the Bànrigh. She called them before her. 'I see many things young Abram: the great past, the mighty present and, sometimes, a little of the eternal future. It was I who called you as you lay asleep on the Pentland Hills. In the giant tapestry of life, my eye sometimes sees threads that meet or join, either by design or a simple knot. Yours I saw, perhaps, because I had something that was rightfully yours.'

'How did you come by it, Your Majesty?'

'Many houses have their brownies, Abram. If something is important and treated carelessly, then a brownie will often take it into care. All it takes to retrieve it is say, "Spirit of home and hearth, reveal unto me that which has been lost," and it will be found. As this was never done, it was brought here for safekeeping. Now it is returned.'

'I mean no disrespect, Your Majesty, but I am curious as to why you did not say you had it.'

'I did. As you lay asleep on the Pentland hills, did I not say to come here and find your heart's desire?'

'Yes, but—'

'I know what you wish to say, Abram. But may I say that something earned under hardship is so much more appreciated than that which comes easily. And besides, are you not now twice blessed?'

'No, Your Majesty.'

The Bànrigh's features hardened, 'No?'

'No, Your Majesty, I am thrice blessed: I have the document of my inheritance, I have the woman I love and,' he paused a moment, 'I have the honour of meeting and knowing the most gracious being that walks these lands.' He bowed low and respectfully.

The hard look remained on her face, 'It takes a brave heart to tease a woman of the Sìth, far less a Bànrigh, Abram Fell. Perhaps I should turn you to a frog.'

Abram laughed, 'Then you would indeed be the Carlin Queen of Cairnsmore.'

'Be off with you before I change my mind,' said the Bànrigh, lightheartedly.

Abram and Katie walked hand-in-hand under a sun-blessed sky on the track to Burnilee, in love with life and with each other. Quite forgetting his anger at Abram, the Laird of Burnilee rejoiced on their return. Some weeks later, after a church wedding, the laird organised a coach to take Abram and Katie to the Borders and the banks of Tweed where they became a laird and his lady.

5

FAERIES AND CHANGELINGS

The faery folk are an unchancy people. If they don't like you, then your life can be made a misery. If they like you, then things can be so much better for you ... or worse. There are many stories of faery folk in Dumfries and Galloway of the Faery Rade when the King and Queen of Elfland ride out on All-Hallows Eve or where a brief visit to elfland can be seven years in the human world or where a child is abducted and a changeling or sìthbheire is left in its place. We shall begin with a grim tale from Hoddam.

TIBBIE'S BAIRNIE

Tibbie Dickson's guidman was gardener to a gentleman and often away from home. One time when he was away Tibbie left the child in the house and went to the well to fetch some water. The well was only fifty yards away so Tibbie thought no harm would come to her bonnie bairnie in the short time she was away. As she returned, Tibbie heard screaming from the house as though someone were poking a pig. She ran to the cradle and such a sight met her eyes. Her bonnie bairnie was gone and in its place was a withered rag of a child, all skin and bone with hands like a mole and a face like a frog. The mouth was a gash that ran from ear to ear and set full centre of the face were two glowering eyes. Was this her child made ill by an evil eye or was it a faery child? To comfort the bairnie, she tried to breastfeed it but it would have none of it. Tibbie tried everything and in the end discovered it preferred porridge, eating as much as two full-grown men in a day. The child never thrived and when others were up and walking it was still abed howling and crying.

Now Tibbie had a few skeins of wool she had spun herself and wanted to go to the weaver to get it made into some fine cloth. With no one to look after her child, she asked her next-door neighbour, Wullie Grieve. Wullie was a tailor and though cursed with a deformity of the spine he was much sought after as a top-class craftsman. Tibbie warned him of the bairn's ill disposition but said he could help himself to her guidman's tobacco as recompense.

Wullie sat by the inglenook, filled his pipe and lit it with a taper. He had barely drawn on the pipe when the child leaped from the bed, scuttled over and whispered in his ear, 'If ye dinnae tell ma mither, I'll play ye a spring on the bagpipes.' Such a fright did Wullie get he near ran from the house, but then he thought to himself, 'Better tae fleetch than tae flyte.' So he said to the bairn, 'Play up ma doo, an I'se tell naebody.' The bairnie leaped back in the cradle and pulled a set of bagpipes from under the straw. Wullie was dazzled by them, covered in ivory, gold, silver and diamonds, as they were. The bairn blew into them until the bag was inflated then began to play, dancing around beside the fascinated tailor. 'This is a thing o Auld Waghorn an gin I sit here an listen mair he'll surely come and rock his ain cradle.' With that Wullie grabbed the bairnie and threw him, bagpipes and all, in to the fire. With a great *whoosh*, the changeling shot up the chimney yelling, 'Deil stick the lousy tailor.'

RIDDLIN IN THE REEK

In the village of Sorbie lived a guidman and his guidwife. More loving, caring parents a child could not have, yet the child they had seemed more demon than human. In frustration they begged advice from a wise old woman, Lucky McRobert, from Kirkinner.

The woman said she would gladly help but they would have to wait until All-Hallow's Eve.

At Halloween, Lucky arrived carrying wood and a riddle and locked the door behind her. She set two stools by the fire, which was on a raised bed in the middle of the floor, and indicated for the husband and wife to sit there. She then lit a candle from her 'etherstane', set it on a candlestick and placed it between the couple. Next she took rowan wood and set it on the fire. As this was being done, the child grew more agitated and finally fled under the bed. Lucky stuck her petticoats into her breeks then dragged the child out and bound it hand and foot with red cloth. She placed it in the riddle and carried it to the fire as it struggled and swore viciously. She held it over the logs and riddled it in the smoke. The child screamed, cursed and spat at Lucky who paid it no attention but kept riddling. It then pleaded with the husband and wife, who sat there horrified but immobile. It then cursed them volubly while the house shook around them. Then, with a scream, the child whirled up in the air and disappeared out of the smoke-hole in the roof.

There was complete silence followed by a gentle knocking on the door and a small voice cried, 'Let me in; I'm wee Tammie.'

THE GUIDWIFE AND THE FAERY

It was early spring, and just outside of Borgue a guidwife was in her washhouse doing her Monday washing, rinsing and wringing the clothes before throwing them into the creel ready for hanging out. Although these were the hunger times, she sang merrily, happy in her work. A knock at the door made her turn around. She was somewhat taken by surprise because there at the door was a tiny, trim woman no more than a foot high. Without a 'by your leave' the wee woman stepped into the washhouse, 'Guidwife,' said she, holding up a wooden coggie, 'hae ye a pickle o meal?'

'Sairy ma dearie, but I hae scant meal fer me and ma bairnies.'

'Gie a pairt o whit ye hae tae a puir body and ye will neer want.'

'Come ben the hoose,' said the good-hearted woman to the wee wifie.

They went indoors and the guidwife opened her meal ark, took the coggie from the woman, filled it and handed it back.

The wee woman looked up at the gudewife and smiled, 'Gin ye neer luik in yer meal ark it'll aye be fu.'

The guidwife turned to place the lid back on the ark. When she turned about the wee woman was gone.

For many a long day she filled her porridge pot with meal from an ark that never faltered. That was until the day her curiosity got the better of her and she had a 'wee keek' inside. From that day she had to fill it herself.

Nurse Kind and Neer Want

A young woman from up the Nith valley was singing and nursing her child when a woman entered the cottage. She wore a faery mantle and carried a tiny girlchild swaddled in a green silk blanket. 'Gie ma bairnie a sook,' said the stranger. The young woman, who was of a kindly disposition, took the child. 'Nurse kind an neer want,' the faery woman said, then instantly disappeared.

Unable to do otherwise, the young lass raised both children with equal love and attention. The faery was true to her word and often when the young woman woke in the morning she would find clothing for both children and delicious food that she herself could eat and that would last without perishing.

At the approach of summer the fairy returned. The child was overjoyed to see its mother, who swept her up in her arms and gently and lovingly stroked her brow. She then turned to the young woman and said, 'Follow me.' The faery set off through a wood and up on to a green hillside which faced the sun. She raised her arm and a door opened on the slope; they entered and the door closed behind. Once inside, the fairy dropped three drops of dew on to the nurse's left eyelid and she saw a land that was blessed with winding streams of silver that flowed among fields of golden corn. The fairy

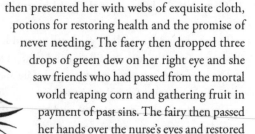

then presented her with webs of exquisite cloth, potions for restoring health and the promise of never needing. The faery then dropped three drops of green dew on her right eye and she saw friends who had passed from the mortal world reaping corn and gathering fruit in payment of past sins. The fairy then passed her hands over the nurse's eyes and restored her ordinary sight. As they left, the nurse noticed the phial of green dew and dropped it into her pouch.

For many years after, the nurse could see the spirits of those who visited the mortal world, until one day she met the faery woman. 'Whit ee dae ye see me wae?'

'Wae baith,' said the nurse. The faery blew in her eyes and the young woman's spirit sight failed.

KING OF THE BROWNIES

It is in the historical record that in the seventeenth century, on the banks of the White Loch of Myrton, on the Machars stood the Castle of Myrton; this was the stronghold of Sir Godfrey McCulloch. Sir Godfrey squandered his inheritance and had to sell it to the Maxwells of Monreith. He then took up residence at Cardoness near Gatehouse of Fleet.

At Cardoness, some of his cattle strayed on to a neighbouring estate owned by William Gordon. Gordon poinded, or impounded, the cattle, presumably until a fee was paid. Sir Godfrey then formed a party to release them and in the process, as the historical record says, 'did shot at the said Gordon with a gun charged, and by the shot broke his thigh-bone and leg, so that he immediately fell to the ground, and within a few hours thereafter died of the same shot wound'. Sir Godfrey fled the country. Some years later he was in Edinburgh and attended church where he was seen by a Galloway man who called out, 'Pit tae the door; there's a murtherer in the kirk!' This was done; Sir Godfrey was arrested, tried and had his head 'stricken frae his body' on 5 March 1697.

The historical record is locally refuted, for when Sir Godfrey was a young man he was at the window of Myrton Castle watching men reroute the castle sewer into the White Loch. He was startled by an apparition appearing beside him. The phantom took on the form of a little old man dressed all in green with white hair and a long white beard. The old man was in a state of wrath. Sir Godfrey remained calm and asked how he could help the stranger. 'I am the King o the Broonies and ma palace is unner the moond on which yer castle staunds. I hae sufferit this wi grace but whit I will no suffer is yer sewer runnin through ma chalmer o dais.'

At once Sir Godfrey ordered the work to be stopped then enquired of His Majesty which direction would be most suitable for the sewer. Thus satisfied, the king promised Sir Godfrey that should he ever be in dire need he would be at his service. So it was that when Sir Godfrey was being carted to the scaffold in Edinburgh the attendant crowd were startled to see an old man on a white horse ride out of Castle Rock and over the surface of Castle Loch towards Sir Godfrey. The condemned man leaped on to the back of the horse, which once more crossed the loch and disappeared back into the rock. When all turned back to the cart, a figure looking just like Sir Godfrey stood there. Unsure of what had just passed the executioner got on with the job and decapitated the prisoner. As his head rolled on the ground, many were heard to whisper, 'It wis no him ava; it wis jist a glamour.'

THE BROWNIE OF DALSWINTON

The Maxwells of Dalswinton, just north of Dumfries, had a brownie. He was devoted to the family and toiled hard in their service, doing the work of ten men. He worked mainly through the night and often kept the servants awake with the noise of his efforts. He was especially devoted to the laird's daughter. In time, she met a young man of whom the brownie approved and was married. In time, she was expecting her first child so the 'cannywife' or midwife was sent for. It was a dark and windy December night and the servant who was supposed to fetch her loitered at his task. This enraged the brownie, who wrapped himself in the lady's cloak, climbed on the waiting horse and set out to collect the midwife. With supernatural ease he crossed the raging River Nith, arriving at the cannywife's house in no time. The woman mounted behind the cloaked rider and they set off back to Dalswinton. She was more than surprised when, instead of going by track and over the bridge, the horse was spurred through muck and mire and across the raging Nith as if it were a metalled road. 'Ride nae by the auld pool,' said the woman, 'lest we meet the broonie.'

'Hae nae fear, dame, ye've met aa the broonies ye'll meet.'

The brownie dropped her at the door then made for the stable. Removing the bridle, he went to the servant lad, who was just pulling on his boots, and thrashed him soundly.

The brownie remained with his beloved mistress until her husband agreed with a minister that he should be baptised. The minister hid in the barn until he appeared – a little, wizened, ancient man – and threw the baptismal water in his face. The brownie vanished instantly, never to return.

MAGGIE'S WELL

Close by Castle Douglas, Maggie sat spinning wool on a rock near the well that to this day bears her name. At the time, she was tending her father's flock of sheep when she happened to look down into the well. From a branch of bog oak a foot below the surface of the water she saw golden chains supporting a giant, golden kettle. Full of excited joy, she ran back to fetch her father and brothers to help pull it out. She had enough wit to mark the spot with her spindle, distaff and tow before she left. She ran in the house and called, 'Faither, faither will ye cam awa tae the well by Bodsknowe and help me puu a pot o gowd I hae seen in it.'

'Ye hae lost yer sense lassie. Dae ye no ken ye hae been glamoured by some elf wha wishes tae droon ye.' Seeing the sad look that came over his daughter, her father laid a tender hand on her shoulder. 'Houts lassie, we'll come wae ye an see whit ferlie ye hae spied.'

When they reached the hillside, Maggie looked for her spindle, distaff and tow, but all she could see was a forest of spindles, distaffs and tow. 'Whit did I tell ye lass. An luik, there are the verra folk o which I spoke.'

Maggie looked in the direction her father had pointed to see a troop of small green-clad figures dancing arm in arm and singing:

Tea an Brandy, Tea an Brandy,
Luik *aboot ye Maggie, Maggie.*   look

With that, they leaped in the air and vanished. All that was left was the fading echo of their laughter. When they looked again, all the spindles, distaffs and tow had disappeared except for Maggie's. When she looked closer she saw her tow had been spun into the finest wool she had ever seen.

THE DANCING PLOUGHMAN

At Enrick Farm just outside of Gatehouse of Fleet was a loch that is now long since drained. On the far side of the loch was a mill that had grown into disrepair. One Halloween, two young ploughmen from the farm went to the smiddy to get their coulters repaired. On the way back, as they passed the mill they heard the sound of music and dancing; fiddlers fiddled and singers sang and all was jollity and merriment. One of the lads decided to go and investigate while his companion waited outside. After some time, the companion looked in the window, saw his friend dancing his heart out and decided to make his way home alone, too tired to take part. The first ploughman never appeared, so a year later on the same day of the week, the companion decided he needed to make the same journey to the smiddy. This time he took the bible with him. On passing the mill, he heard the same music and dancing and ventured to look in. There he saw his friend dancing away as he had done twelve months earlier. He entered and handed the dancer his bible. Instantly the lights went out, the music stopped and the mill was deserted. For the dancing ploughman, no time had passed.

THE FAERY BOY

There was once a boy by the name of John Williamson whose father, a packman, was drowned returning from Ireland. Consequently, the boy was raised by his mother and grandfather. The grandfather, whose name was Sproat, lived in Borgue. Soon afterwards, the boy began to disappear for days at a time, sometimes a week. Where he went, he would never disclose, but rumour had it that he was away with the faeries.

The Laird of Barmagachan was out cutting peats assisted by some neighbours. At dinnertime they were sitting in a circle eating bread and cheese when the boy appeared among them. 'Johnny, whaur did ye come frae?' said one of the company.

'I cam wae oor folks.'

'Yer folks; wha are they?'

'Ye see yon hole whaur the barrow is coupit? That's whaur I cam frae.'

An old man by the name of Brown took the boy home and advised his grandfather to visit a Papist priest who would give him something that would keep away the faery folk. When he returned home, he was wearing a black ribbon round his neck on which hung a cross. Old Brown and the grandfather were promptly excommunicated by the local minister and kirk session: they accepted the presence of faeries but would have no truck with Papists.

6

JOHN THE FISHERMAN

Up until the 1690s, Old John and Old Janet had lived a long and good life in a tiny cottage at Carsluith just east of Ferrytown of Cree. They had been together since they were children and were devoted, faithful and true to each other through bad times and worse. But now the Seven Ill Years of the Starvation Times were upon them and hunger was everywhere. Harvests had failed because of the continual rains, crops rotted in the fields and people were forced to dig up wild roots to ease the wracking hunger pains; in almost every family death through malnutrition was now common. John and Janet had longed for children but were now thankful that they did not have to endure the sight of their children dying. Although they suffered badly they had managed to contain their suffering with fish, shellfish and seaweed, but now the weather had turned to continuous storms and John could catch nothing. Going out on his boat was too dangerous so he was resigned to pegging down his creels on the mudflats at low tide and fishing from the shore. He caught nothing.

Day after day, John faithfully took his creels down to the Cree estuary at low tide and returned at the next low to find them empty. Each time he returned wet and chilled to a damp, cold house, for all their peat and bundles of sticks had been soaked through. Everyone has their breaking point and this was John's. He sat beside Janet on the bed and said, 'Oor fire's oot an we huv nae meat in the hoose. Whit are we tae dae? The neichbours are as bad aff as we be, sae they cannae help.' He tenderly took Janet's face in his hands, 'I am gaun doon yae last time. If I catch nothin, I am gaun tae cast masel i the sea; fer I will no gang through this langsome daith.' He leaned forward and kissed her brow. 'If I dinnae return by the gloamin, tak the rope frae unner the eaves, mak a noose then staun on that stuil and tie it aboot that beam abuin yer heid, put it aboot your craig then kick awa the stuil. If Guid Lord taks mercy on us, I wull see ye in heaven. If no, I'll see ye in Hell. It cannae be worse than this.'

Janet threw her arms about her beloved husband, 'I wull dae that John, for I cuildnae bear tae leeve withoot ye. I trust us baith tae Providence.'

They held each other close, then John pulled away and walked out the door without another word. Janet sat on the bed quietly weeping. The fisherman gathered up his creels, a bucket of putrid fish guts and heads and hauled them to the boat. He pushed it into water and rowed out into the estuary which runs north to south. The wind was from the west and was throwing up breakers in the usually quiet water. The boat rose and slammed down with bone-jarring impact. Eventually he was midstream and let the flow carry him out. Then, with the wind behind, he rowed until he was opposite Cairnhallaig. There he scooped heads and guts into each creel and dropped them and their markers over the side before rowing on a little further to fish with a longline. John dropped his anchorstone over the side, baited his six hooks and threw the weighted line into the sea. He sat hunched under his oilskin as the wind continued to fill the boat with spray. His only activity was using an old coggie to empty out the water. Due to his advanced hunger he began to chill and had no alternative but to pull in the lines. There was nothing. He hauled in the anchorstone then removed the weight from the line and let it out again before rowing back to the creels with the line dragging behind. The journey was one of pure misery as he fought against the wind. It took him an age to cover a few hundred yards to the creels. When he pulled them up they were all empty as were the hooks on the longline. He rebaited the hooks then, in aching despair, fought his way back home. As he hit the shore he checked the line but there was nothing. It was the end. John dragged the boat ashore – at least someone in the future might make good use of it. A hundred yards further on, a fellow fisherman and his son had built a rough jetty of large granite boulders. He would throw himself into deep water from there and his body would be carried out to sea, never to be seen again.

As John trudged along the beach he noticed a finely dressed man walking towards him. The stranger seemed oblivious to and unaffected by the stormy conditions. As he drew closer John was fascinated by his clothing, so inappropriate for the country and the conditions. He wore fine-grained, green, buckled shoes; green silk stockings; pleated, scarlet silk breeches; with a matching coat. At his neck was a white cravat that seemed to explode out of the coat. His black, curled wig hung thick over his shoulders and set on top was a wide, green, broad-brimmed hat, round which was tied a scarlet, bowed ribbon. The man's face was strangely pale and defined by a well-trimmed black moustache and goatee beard. What fascinated the fisherman was that the man's hat and clothes seemed unaffected by the hard wind, whereas he was continually buffeted. 'Greetings, friend,' said the stranger. 'You seem a little melancholy today. What is the matter?'

His tone was slightly imperious but to John seemed affable enough. 'Oh sir, I wuidnae bother ye wae ma troubles.'

'Why?' asked the stranger.

'There's nocht ye cuid dae aboot it.'

'Do not be so sure, my man,
There may be some way that I can
relieve you of your troubles.'

John was sure the man could do
nothing for him, but his interest in him
at least demanded a reply. 'Weel, sir,
it is this: ma guidwife and I hae been
marryit for mony years an we are, if
you dinnae mynd me saying this o
a couple in oor advanced years,
devoted tae each ither.'

'As it should be, my man. But why the melancholy?'

'Well, these ill years hae servit naebody weel, least o aa oorsels. Oor theik is leakin, aa the peat an sticks are soakit and warst o aa is that I huvnae pit meat on oor table. Sae Janet, that's ma guidwife, an I are stervin.' John looked into the deep black eyes of the stranger and sighed, 'It's this, sir. I telt Janet if I didnae cam back by the gloamin it wis acuase I wis deep droont in the sea. That bein the case, she wis tae hing herself.'

'That will not do at all,' said the man.

'Sae whit dae ye think we suid dae?'

'What I think is that were you to give me the gift I ask, then I would lay to rest all your troubles. Perhaps make you the richest man in Galloway.'

John gave a pathetic laugh, 'I dinnae need that, sir, juist gettin us past these ill times wuid be eneuch.' He held his arms up in protest, 'But there is naethin that I hae that ye wuid wish fer.'

'I will be the judge of that, my good man,' the stranger said, amiably.

'As long as ye dinnae ask fer ma guidwife, ye can hae whit ye like.

'As pleasant a woman as I'm sure your wife is, I would not ask that of you.'

'In that case sir, as lang as ye ask it in decency, ye can hae whit ye wish.'

'It's a simple request. All I wish is your first-born son.'

'I am a simple man, sir, but I dinnae tak kindly tae folk teaslin me.'

'Why, sir,' said the man, rising up to his full height, seemingly offended, 'I never tease.'

'I didnae mean tae offend, but ye can see that I am advanced in years and ma wife is tae. We've been mairryit whit seems a hunner years and the Guid Lord has nae seen fit tae bless us wi weans.'

The man seemed to shudder at the mention of the Almighty, 'Yes, well, that is my wish. When he reaches the age of eighteen you will bring him to me at this very spot. If you agree to this I will bring you wealth and servants to care for you and your wife.'

'I'll dae it,' said John, still unsure if he was being teased. 'Easy eneuch tae hecht that.'

'When he is eighteen I want him brought to me right here.'

'Indeed I wull dae that, sir; on the verra day o the lad's aichteenth birthday, at this verra time.'

The stranger smiled, 'Do you know what to do now?'

'I wis hopin tae gaither ma riches.'

'In that case John, gather up your fishing lines and cast them in the water; and don't bother baiting them.'

John walked back to his boat and lifted the seat at the rear under which he stored his longlines. He removed one and threw it in the water. It had barely sunk beneath the surface when the line tugged furiously. John pulled out half a dozen large cod. These he dropped into the boat. Next catch was mackerel, followed by bass, then pollock. Every cast produced a full haul until the boat was over half full. Though exhilarated, exhaustion and bleeding hands made him stop. 'That's mair than eneuch,' he said. 'Noo I'll be able tae sell them tae oor neichbours wha are aa stervin as weel. Ye're richt, sir, we'll be rich.'

'Yes, well, just hold on there John. There's something you and your wife have to do before that.'

'And whit wuid that be sir?'

'You must first cut off their heads, gut and clean them.'

'As ye say, sir, but folk are no keen on peyin money fer heidless fish. Whit are they tae mak their soup wi? Still I am obleegit fer yer kind advice.'

'It's not kind advice, John. You must!'

'Then I wull, sir, and thank ye.'

'Good.'

John loaded fish into his creel then turned to thank the well-dressed stranger, but he had disappeared. Puzzled at the sudden departure of his benefactor, he plodded back to the house almost bent double with the weight of fish and was only just in time; mirk was settling as he approached the front door. Janet was already on the stool and was tying the grass rope round the beam when, through the window, she saw the easily recognisable figure of her husband. She climbed off the stool and opened the door. John stooped to enter and as he did so a large cod slid over his shoulder and on to the floor, 'Gracious me, John, that's a muckle fish ye hae there.'

'Aye Janet, an a basket fuu o them. Aye, an the boat half fuu forbye.'

'We'll be leevin like gentry,' said Janet.

'Maybe no sae grand, lass, but a guy bit mair prosperous than we huv been in years. Noo get anither creel an help me cairry them up tae the hoose.'

They emptied the boat and carried all the fish into the house where they laid them on old grass mats. 'The mannie thet telt me whaur tae fling ma lines said we need tae tak aff the heids and gut an clean them.'

'He must hae been an awfu guid man. A bit like Jesus wi the fishermen on the sea o Galilea.'

'Aye, I suppose it's the same. Weel, the Lord's blessin on the chiel.'

Janet sharpened their knives on a whetstone then they began to decapitate and gut the fish. No sooner were the heads off than gold, silver and diamonds poured from inside them on to the floor. Both jaws fell open in surprise. They looked at each other then furiously began to chop heads. Each time a fistful of gold or silver or precious stones scattered about their feet. In time, one side of the room was awash with fish and fishheads, the other was piled up with a small mountain of treasure.

'I tak back whit I said, hen: we wull leeve like gentry. It's a miracle. I wish I cuid shak that man's haun the noo.'

'Aye, an I micht even gie him a kiss on the cheik.'

'I'd gie him wan masel,' said John. They both burst into fits of laughter before getting up and dancing a reel. Both slipped and fell headlong among the fish where they lay screaming with glee. Exhausted, they fell onto their bed and slept soundly.

After a breakfast of mackerel they tidied up their horde and hid it beneath their bed. They then hired a cart from a nearby farmer in exchange for a bucket of fish then travelled round the district distributing the fish for free to the starving population, giving extra to the elderly and families with small children – many a grateful prayer was said for them that night. As they travelled they discussed the stranger, 'He did say mair than juist whaur tae fling the line lass, but I'm no gaun tae tell ye acause ye micht think we wur baith gyte.'

'Weel, that is yer decision, John, an I wull respect that.'

After burying their treasure they took a large pouchfull with them to Kirkcudbright and set about buying themselves a large cottage with seven acres of land and three servants. John kept his boat and creels and displayed them at the front door of the cottage to remind him of his hard work and good fortune. They were a year and a day in the cottage when, to everyone's surprise – not least of all John's – Janet gave birth to a son. He was also christened John. He was a bonny baby and grew into a strong intelligent boy. They hired a tutor and bought a library of books then set up a school room in a nearby cottage to ensure the lad and other children in the district were well educated. They also made sure that young John was skilled in boatmanship and husbandry, so that he had brawn as well as brain.

John and Janet nurtured their son and gave him all the love and care a father and mother should. The Seven Ill Years of the Starvation Times were over and prosperity returned to the area. But no one ever begrudged John and Janet their good fortune; all felt it was God's gift for their generosity in the hard times. Although wealthy, John still took his son out laying creels and longlining and it was on one of those occasions which happened to be the boy's seventeenth birthday that the words of the stranger returned, 'When he is eighteen I want him brought to me right here.' He remembered the despair of starvation, the desperate desire to save his beloved Janet – he would have agreed to walk through the fires of hell. Now it seemed he would have to do worse. The old fisherman slipped into melancholy. Young John grew ever more worried for his father as each time he returned from school his father seemed ever deeper in despair. Janet would see him pacing back and forward, talking as if to some invisible presence. She asked if she or young John had offended him. He just shook his head.

'Whit is wrong wi him, Johnnie? When ye are at schuil he neer talks tae me. He juist sits in his chair an does naethin. Are ye suir ye havnae vexed him?'

'I'm suir, Mither.'

'We'll ask him the nicht when ye cam hame frae schuil.'

Mother and son confronted old John just after young John returned from school at half past six. 'John, I hae been yer wife fer a lang time and I hae din ma best by ye. But noo I wis wunnerin if masel or wee John here had assaultit ye?'

'Ye mean *insultit*, mither,' interrupted Johnnie.

'That's whit I said!'

'I ken whit ye mean, hen, an no, it is no yer faut. Ye've aye been the best wife ony man cuid wish fer. It is me. I kept sumthin back frae ye.'

'That's no like you, John. Whit wis it?'

'I did say at the time. It wis when we hud aa they fish that wur fuu of gowd and the likes. I said that a fella hud helped me.'

'Aye, I mynd noo. Ye said there wis something ye wernae gaun tae tell me.'

'I agreed with the fella that he cuid have onything he wantit frae me, as lang as it wis no yersel.'

'So whit did he want?'

'He said ma first born son.'

Janet's hands went up to her mouth in horror, 'Oh, John, whit huv ye duin?'

John shook his head in despair. 'I dinae ken that we wuid hae a laddie. I mean, we wur weel past the age an it seemit sic a rideeculous request that I agreed.'

'An when is this wicht comin tae claim oor son?'

'On his aichteenth birthday at aboot fower o the clock, doon whaur we keppit the boat.'

Johnnie stood up, pulled his bonnet from his head and bowed deeply to his father, 'I am yer obedient son and I am maist grateful tae hae ye an mither as ma paurants. I jalouse that hud ye no makit that greeance I wid no be here. A pact wi the Deil it micht hae been, but ill will no come o it.'

'Whit dae ye mean a pact wi the Deil?' said Janet.

'I'm thinkin that if it wisnae Auld Clootie it wid be wan o his myrmidons,' said Johnnie.

'God preserve us,' said Janet.

Even Old John was shocked, never having thought it all through. 'He micht be the Deil, but I am man o honour an I hae tae keep ma word.'

'John!' exclaimed Janet. 'Whit honour is there in haunin yer ain son ower tae the Deil.'

'Haud on, mither. Ma faither is an honourable man an he maun dae whit he maun dae. That disnae mean I hae tae agree wi it.'

'Ye cannae best the Deil, son,' said his mother, tears streaming down her face.

'Yer mither's richt, son.' Old John sat in his chair and could barely stop the tears as they trickled down his grizzled face.

Young John smiled at his parents, 'A lad cuidnae ask fer better paurants than yersels. Ye did yer best by me, ye lued me, ye cared fer me and ye gied me the best schuilin in mony mair weys than yin. Weel, I am gaun tae uise that schuilin tae sort this oot. Noo here's whit I want fer ma birthday.'

The day of Johnnie's birthday arrived and father and mother were beside themselves with grief. Old John tried his best to contain it, but the occasional trickle of tears told another tale. Janet spent her time fussing over Johnnie, who did his best to calm her. Just before midday a horse and cart arrived from Campbell, the carpenter in Kirkcudbright. Johnnie went out and asked the driver if he could deliver it further down the track to a place on the beach. He accompanied the driver.

As the fateful hour approached Johnnie remained calm and asked his parents to get their bibles and for his father to lead them to the shore. Johnnie gathered up his bible and a walking stick and set out behind his father. He himself took his mother's arm; partly to hold her in case she fainted. When they arrived there were three chairs and a table waiting for them. Johnnie sat his mother down in the middle and beckoned his father to the seat on the right facing the estuary. He set his bible on the table and bid them to do the same. From his coat pocket he removed a small silver flask and a silver quaich. He poured a small quantity of sherry into the quaich and held it up to his parents. 'This day I am become a man, an am truly blessit wi the finest paurants ony man cuid hae. Here's tae ye an the next aichteen years.' He took a small sip. Janet howled and Old John let the tears flood from his eyes. Johnnie tenderly took his mother's left hand and placed the quaich in it. 'Drink ma halth, Mither.' Janet contained her grief and took a small sip. Johnnie passed it to his father who did the same. He then held the quaich up to the sky, noting the way it reflected the dazzling, amber sun as it set. 'And here's tae Aamichty God and his belovit son Jesus Christ wha saicrifeecit himsel on the cross so that we micht be savit.'

'Amen,' they chorused. Each in turn took another small sip and the quaich was empty. Johnnie placed the flask and quaich back in his pocket. He then took his stick and drew a circle about them in the shell-grit sand, at the same time reciting the Lord's Prayer, then sat down. He leaned forward, picked up the bibles and handed each their own. 'I think it wuid be a grand idea if we read oor favourit piece frae the Guid Book. Mither, ye stert.'

For a while each read their favourite piece then second favourite until Johnny noticed a figure approaching. 'Wuid this be the chiel ye were expectin, Faither?'

Old John turned and looked over his right shoulder. He felt a cold hand claw at his heart. 'Aye son, tis he.'

Janet turned away, unable to look on the fiend.

'I have come,' said the man to Old John.

'What have ye come fer?' asked Johnnie.

'I have come for you,' said the stranger, stabbing a finger at Johnnie. 'You are my property. I paid for you before you were begotten or born.'

'I am ma faither's an ma mither's son and I am certainly naebody's gear, except perhaps Aamichty God.'

The stranger's face flushed in fury, 'Do you know who I am?'

'I care little wha ye are if ye wuid dare enslave a freeborn body. Aye, an I care less fer onybody wha wuid daur enslave an immortal saul.'

The stranger drew himself up to his full height, seeming to blot out the sky. Janet and John cowered in their chairs but Johnnie faced down the onslaught, 'If ye want me, then ye maun cam an tak me; if you daur.' The young man opened his bible and began to read aloud from the Gospel of St John, 'In the beginning was the Word, and the Word was with God, and the Word was God.' The stranger stepped forward to grab Johnnie, but as his foot crossed the line scored in the sand he gave a howl of pain and retreated. Johnnie kept reading, 'The same was in the beginning with God.' The fiend now moved round the circle where Johnnie was closest and made a grab for the lad. The arm of his coat dissolved, exposing a scaly arm. He howled in pain and rage and withdrew. Johnnie read on, 'All things were made by him; and without him was not anything made that was made.' He looked up from the book and quoted verse four directly at the stranger, 'In him was life; and the life was the light of men.'

In that instant, the beast's clothing dissolved entirely leaving him exposed for who he was. 'Begone Satan! Ye hae na pooer ower me or ma faimily. Begone!'

The creature roared with ferocity, turned and ran into the estuary, flames erupting about him. In the middle of the current, he sank beneath the surface. The water boiled and great clouds of steam rose high into the sky. Slowly the gentle flow of the river carried away the disturbance and a soft wind dispersed the vapour. Johnnie stood up and laid his bible on the table and took out the flask and quaich, 'A wee toast afore we gang hame?'

The Strange Visitor

A wifie was sitting at her reel one night;
And still she sat, and still she reeled, and still she wished for company.
In came a pair of broad broad soles, and sat down at the fireside;
And still she sat, and still she reeled, and still she wished for company.
In came a pair of small small legs, and sat down on the broad broad soles;
And still she sat, and still she reeled, and still she wished for company.
In came a pair of thick thick knees, and sat down on the small small small legs;
And still she sat, and still she reeled, and still she wished for company.
In came a pair of thin thin thighs, and sat down on the thick thick knees;
And still she sat, and still she reeled, and still she wished for company.
In came a pair of huge huge hips, and sat down on the thin thin thighs;
And still she sat, and still she reeled, and still she wished for company.
In came a wee wee waist, and sat down on the huge huge hips;
And still she sat, and still she reeled, and still she wished for company.
In came a pair of broad broad shoulders, and sat down on the wee wee waist;
And still she sat, and still she reeled, and still she wished for company.
In came a pair of small small arms, and sat down on the broad broad shoulders;

And still she sat, and still she reeled, and still she wished for company.
In came a pair of huge huge hands, and sat down on the small small arms;
And still she sat, and still she reeled, and still she wished for company.
In came a small small neck, and sat down on the broad broad shoulders;
And still she sat, and still she reeled, and still she wished for company.
In came a huge huge head, and sat down on the small small neck.
'How did you get such broad broad feet?' quoth the woman.
'Much tramping, much tramping' (gruffly).
'How did you get such small small legs?'
'Aih-h-h!–late–and wee-e-e–moul' (whiningly).
'How did you get such thick thick knees?'
'Much praying, much praying' (piously);
'How did you get such thin thin thighs?'
'Aih-h-h!–late–and wee-e-e–moul' (whiningly).
'How did you get such big big hips?'
'Much sitting, much sitting' (gruffly).
'How did you get such a wee wee waist?'
'Aih-h-h!–late–and wee-e-e–moul' (whiningly).
'How did you get such broad broad shoulders?'
'With carrying broom, with carrying broom' (gruffly).
'How did you get such small small arms?'
'Aih-h-h!–late–and we-e-e–moul' (whiningly).
'How did you get such huge huge hands?'
'Threshing with an iron flail, threshing with an iron flail' (gruffly).
'How did you get such a small small neck?'
'Aih-h-h!–late–wee-e-e–moul' (pitifully).
'How did you get such a huge huge head?'
'Much knowledge, much knowledge' (keenly).
'What do you come for?'
'For you !' (At the top of the voice, with a wave of the arm, and a stamp of the feet.)

7

HOO TAE DEAL
WI THE DEIL

Scotland has always had a strange relationship with the Devil. Not only is he feared, he is also respected. Perhaps because he is a fallen angel and otherwise part of God's great plan – he being God, would he let such an evil creature exist if not as part of a grand design: to make humanity worthy of redemption, perhaps?

One man, reputed to have met Auld Clootie, replied that he was 'a gey decent chiel'. Here, we 'gie the Deil his due'. There was land set aside on any farm called a 'feart place', where things were allowed to grow wild. It was generally known as the 'Guidman's Croft', a propitiation to the Devil (nowadays you get a farming subsidy). Here the Devil could be found in various disguises: a black ram, a black dog, a brindled cat or a goat. On a Friday, a goat could pay him a visit to get his or her beard trimmed.

Should you have the mischance to meet him, here are a couple of ways to 'deal wi the Deil'.

ADAM FORRESTER AND THE CIRCLE OF STEEL

In the village of St John's town of Dalry, otherwise known as the Clachan of Dalry, there stood an inn. Around 1680 the hostelry was run by a howdie or midwife called Lucky Hare – Lucky, in the

hope that she would safely deliver your child, and
Hare because she was thought to have witchy
inclinations, for it was said that witches
loved to shapeshift into hares
for their covens or meetings.

A little way from Dalry
at Knocksheen, the hill of
the fairy folk, lived Adam
Forrester, a hard-working,
hard-drinking farmer. On
an evening, Adam would
mount his old nag and ride down the
Garroch Burn, across the ford on the river
Ken, across the haugh or flatland beside the river,
up past the old kirk to the inn, tether his horse to
a ring on the wall and enter. 'Lucky Hare, it's your
lucky night, Adam is here. Gie's a kiss.'

'Naw! I'm no kissin a smelly auld fermer wha stinks o coos.'

'Ah weel, gie's a whisky an a beer ... an a beer and a whisky ...'
Until he was roaring-drunk full.

'Ye ken somethin, Lucky?' he would say, leaning a little
unsteadily on the bar. 'Ye neer seem tae get aulder.' Lucky just
nodded. He would lean forward, conspiratorially, and in slightly
hushed tones, say, 'I think ye are a carlin. I think that the Deil is
keepin ye young.'

'Aye, that'll be richt,' she would reply dismissively.

He would then ride home, facing backwards on the saddle, to
allow him to sleep, in his drink-induced stupor, on the rump of
the horse – the luckless beast knowing its way home.

It was a Friday night and when Adam finished his work he
mounted his nag, rode down the Garroch Burn, across the ford,
across the haugh, up past the kirk to the Clachan Inn. He tied the
reins to the ring and entered, 'Lucky Hare, it's your lucky night,
hen, Adam is here. Gie's a kiss.'

'Naw!'

'Weel, gie me a whisky an a beer.'

'Naw!'

'How no? Whit hae I duin?'

'Nuthin. I'm gaun oot.'

'Whaur ye gaun?'

'Nane o yer business.'

'Please yersel. Cheerio. Jimmy, gie's a whisky an a beer … an a beer an a whisky …' Until he was roaring-drunk full.

At the midnight hour Adam staggered for the door, untethered his nag and mounted the wrong way: forward. 'Ach! Never mind,' he said, urging the horse on. Distantly he heard the sound of pipes. As he passed the kirk he noticed a candle burning in the window of the now-disused building, from where also came the frantic music. 'A ceilidh? I fancy a wee bit o that,' he said, dismounting and tying the reins to a bush. He swayed towards the window and gripping the sill hoisted himself to have a peek in. There in front of him, in full flight, danced the howdie. 'Oh man! It's Lucky Hare.' He glanced briefly to her right and there dancing like teenagers were Auld Jock and Auld Jean. Well into their eighties, they danced a wild and sprightly Highland Scottische. 'I thocht as much, they're aa carlins; witches.'

To their left danced beasties, bogles, ghaisties, wraiths, witches and their like; and in the corner, dancing a jig to his own pipes, black, hairy, with horns and a forky tail, was Auld Hornie, Auld Clootie: the very Devil himself.

'Ooh! It's the witches' Sabbat,' wailed a quivering Adam. 'Ach! But there's Lucky Hare.'

The sight of his love and desire gave him courage and he yelled out, 'Ye cannae deny it noo, Lucky. Sae gie's a kiss.'

In an instant the lights went out and the door was dragged open; out rushed the Hellish legion, all fury and menace, 'We're gaun to get ye, Adam Forrester. We're going to stick a muckle fork in ye an burn ye in the fires o Hell.'

'Oh no ye're no,' howled Adam, suddenly sobering and leaping for his horse. He grabbed the reins off the bush and catapulted on the saddle and, for the first time in its life, gave the horse's rump a mighty thwack. The startled nag shot off homeward, leaving the

Satanic host in its wake. Just as quickly, the demons recovered and made chase, their supernatural powers giving the advantage. The terrified Adam again slapped the beast, whose own fear forced her to greater effort. Adam knew that if they could but cross the ford they would be safe, knowing full well that the beasts of Hell cannot cross over sacred running water. An instant from disaster the horse made the ford, passing so quickly through the river that she barely wet her fetlocks.

Safely on the opposite bank, Adam turned his steed and, with a thumb to his nose, yelled:

'Ha, ha, ha; hee, hee, hee;
Ye cannae catch me fer a wee bumbee.'

The devilish crew stood a moment glaring at Adam before turning south and rushing down the river.

'Whaur are they gaun?' said Adam to no one. As he stood watching, the unholy legion reached the bridge at New Galloway and crossed over.

He wasn't expecting that. With a strangled scream he turned the horse. She needed no urging and dashed off homewards. Adam soon realised that he would never make it and decided on a shortcut over Waterside Hill. The horse made the slopes and did her best to gallop to the top. Unfortunately, she was an old horse and Lucky Hare was soon upon her. Grabbing the nag's tail the witch slapped the rear end of the horse, leaving a handprint that was there to the end of its life. Shock and fear caused the horse to bound in one graceful leap to the top of the hill. Alas, too late, the Devil and his cohort had surrounded them. As they advanced upwards they chanted, 'We're gaun to get ye. We're gaun to get ye.'

But Adam was a Galloway man from an ancient Galloway family who had suffered and survived centuries of invasion and persecution, a people who readily raised their sword in attack and defence. And so it was that Adam leaped from the saddle and drew his good sword. Laughter ran through the horde. 'What use is a puny sword against the Earl of Hell?' called out Lucky Hare.

'We shall see,' said Adam, plunging the point into the turf in front of him. Holding the top of the blade in both hands so tightly his palms bled, he dragged the blade through the turf until the score surrounded them. He then raised the sword to form the sign of the cross and yelled, 'A curse on ony beast, bogle, ghaist, wraith, carlin or Deil that dares pass God's holy circle o steel.' Adam then put his arms around the neck of his beloved horse to hold her within the sacred precinct. 'Steady, lass, steady,' he cooed to calm the agitated animal ... and himself.

All night the demonic beasts sallied against Adam and each time were repelled by God's holy protection, until, 'cock a dooddle doo,' a cockerel crowed the coming dawn. With a rush and a roar the hillside opened and Adam's tormentors disappeared back to Hell. They could not take Adam, so instead they took Lucky Hare: never seen again.

As for Adam and his faithful nag, they rode home to the safety of their homely, sacred rowan tree and from that day forward the old farmer never touched another drop of drink.

THE ROPE OF SAND

Michael Scott was a magician, so they said. A canny man with an enquiring mind, his reputation would, in time, be known as far away as Paris and Rome. For the moment, at least, he was happily raising a family on the shore at Glenluce. Just above the beach he built a wee butt and ben, a two-roomed, thatched cottage: one room for the animals and one for himself and his family. Though he was delighted with his workmanship, his wife expressed her disappointment that he had not built a chimney. Michael protested that a fire on the floor was best as it kept the thatch dry and prevented rain dripping through. His wife was unimpressed. She was also unimpressed that Michael, who had been well paid for curing the Lord of Galloway of a strange affliction, had taken to drinking more than usual with the proceeds. Things came to a head and she departed to her mother's house, taking their seven children with them. Michael followed them pleading with his wife, 'Please come hame, Peggy.'

'No until ye stop the drinkin,' replied his long-suffering wife, 'Ye are a guid man, Michael Scott, but a bad influence on these bonny bairns o yers.'

Michael had enjoyed his drink, feeling it was a just reward for all his long hours of study. Now he was in a dilemma: the need to do right by his family, but a growing taste for drink. He pondered long, then chastised himself for doing just that. 'When ye hae to tak time to consider whether drink or yer faimily is maist important, ye hae lost your senses, Michael.' From that moment he never touched another drop of drink for the rest of his life.

With a new resolve, he visited his wife, told her of his decision and asked her to return home.

'Ae week, Michael? I think we'll need a wee bittie langer than that. Six months maybe?'

'Whit? Six months?'

'Aye. Ye ken whit they say, Michael, "Mony a promise made in the storm; forgotten in the calm." Eh?'

Michael retreated, feeling truly admonished. A day later he had a plan: he would build a chimney and decorate their home with curtains, a large table with nine chairs and a sideboard, with china and real metal cutlery instead of the usual wooden bowls and horn spoons. In two weeks all was done. His delight was to hang their great cauldron from a hook in the chimney: he would prepare a grand stew for his family's homecoming. Full of expectation and joy, he rushed off to see his wife.

'Six months, Michael!'

A dejected Michael trailed back home, head bowed. As he trudged up the path to his house he heard a manic laugh from above him. He looked towards his newly built chimney and there on top sat a wee devil picking out a pointy ear with his forky tail. Michael gave his head a shake, 'Thocht I wis aff the effects o the drink.' He reached the door, lifted the latch and stepped inside. His heart sank. The place was a complete mess: curtains pulled from the windows, tables and chairs up-ended and the sideboard on its face in a sea of broken dishes, and, to add insult to injury, the ashes from the fire were scattered over everything. Down the chimney came a demented laugh; Michael almost cried. Then it dawned on him what was the problem: some time before Michael had halted a plague by challenging the Devil to a piping competition. The Devil had accepted, knowing full well that he was the greatest piper in Creation. However, the Devil is not a Scotsman and did not know that Scots folk are truly the greatest pipers. The Devil lost, and being a lousy loser, he was now getting his revenge.

Michael righted a chair and sat down, elbow on knee, chin on hand. For a while he pondered; then a determination took over, 'Nae yin is gaun tae beat me or prevent me gettin my faimily back. No even Satan himsel, or ma name is no Michael Scott.'

Michael rehung the curtains, righted the table, chairs and sideboard then replaced the dishes, throwing out those too damaged to repair. He dusted down the house, rehung the cauldron, made his supper, ate it and went to bed.

Next day, he was up early to start work on creating a garden for the house, where he would not only grow vegetable but decorate it with foxgloves, heather and honeysuckle. He then went into Glenluce to order more dishes. On his return he was greeted by the cackling imp. Steeling himself, he entered the house and was confronted with the same mess. Patiently he cleared up, had his supper and went to bed. Day after day, the same scene was played out until one evening, having made his supper of porridge oats, he gazed in the pot and realised, as often happens with porridge, that he had made too much. He hated wasting it, but also had a distaste of cold porridge. He also hated dining alone so had the idea of inviting the wee devil. He removed the cauldron and shouted up the chimney, 'Hello!'

'Hello!' came the high-pitched reply.

'Would ye like a wee bit porridge?'

'Aye.'

'Come on doon then.'

The devil scuttered down the chimney, across the floor and leaped on to a chair. Michael spooned the remaining porridge into a wooden bowl laid it in front of the imp and handed him a horn spoon. 'No point in chancing another breakage,' he thought.

The denizen of Hell noisily gulped down the porridge. 'Did ye enjoy that?' asked Michael, genuinely interested in the eating habits of demons and the like.

'Aye!' said the devil, with a satisfied grin.

Michael nodded and smiled, 'So, are ye steying lang?'

'Aye!'

'Really?'

'Aye!'

'How long?'

'How auld are ye?'

'Thirty-five,' said Michael, pulling his shoulders back and drawing in his stomach.

'An yer faither?'

'Seeventy.'

'Probably anither thirty-five years.'

'Thirty-five years!' exclaimed Michael, his voice rising an octave. He did a quick calculation on his fingers as to the days he might suffer, 'Three hundred and sixty-five times thirty-five is … a lot,' he said.

'Aye!'

'Can ye no juist gang awa and lea me in peace? I hae troubles eneuch.'

'Naw!'

'Why no?'

'It's mair than ma job's worth. His lairdship would stick a fork in me and toast me in the fires o Hell.'

Michael winced, 'Nasty.'

The wee devil nodded, his teeth gritted and eyes wide.

'Is there nae wey I can get rid o ye?'

'Nawwww …' He paused. 'Wwweel, aye. But it's no worth tryin,' he added.

'What's no worth tryin?'

'Well, if ye ask me tae dae somethin an I cannae dae it, then I hae tae gang back tae Hell. But it's no worth it, acause I can dae onythin.'

'Hoo mony goes dae I get?' asked Michael, raising a brow.

'Three.'

'Three! I thocht that,' said Michael, his voice rising with interest. 'Mmm.'

'Aye!' said the devil, cocking his head to the one side, leaning forward on one elbow and a look of challenge on his face.

Michael took a moment then said, 'Get me a bag o gowd.'

'That's easy.'

'Ye cannae steal it.'

'Ooh! That's mair difficult.' The wee imp's red eyes disappeared inside his head for a moment, then 'Ah!' he exclaimed, rushing out the door. He scuttered over the Galloway hills until he found an ancient Stone Age chamber, hauled back the rock and pulled out a hoard of gold. Wrapping the treasure in an old, dead rabbit skin, he sped back to the cottage and slapped it down on the table, 'There ye go!'

'Och!' exclaimed Michael, 'Ye beat me.'

'Aye!' said the imp with a smug grin.

'I better pit it awa oot o sicht,' said Michael, opening a door on the sideboard, the flicker of a grin passing over his face.

'Micht be a guid idea,' said the wee devil.

'Twa tae gang,' said Michael, thoughtfully looking up at the beams he had scrubbed clean of soot. 'Ye ken, I've ayeweys fancied daein a wee bit of sea-fishin and ma boys are aye on at me tae get a boat.'

'A boat? I thocht ye wuid think o somethin mair difficult than that.'

'There's mair,' said Michael. 'Ye cannae big it or steal it and it has tae be new.'

'Noo that is hard.' The devil sat for a long time lost in thought, his eyes once again back to front. With an audible *slap* the eyes flopped back into place, a grin of triumph crossed his face and he leaped in the air. Without so much as touching the ground he shot through the partially open door in the direction of the beach. Michael followed in time to see him shooting across the wet sand of low tide and diving into Luce Bay. He followed the rapidly growing white wake as the beastie swam out into the Solway Firth in the direction of the Isle of Man. As Michael paced across the half-mile-wide sand the imp was cruising into the Irish Sea where he abruptly dived to the bottom. There he found a brand new fishing boat, sunk in a storm. The fortunate crew had made their lifeboat and reached the Isle of Man. The vessel was now 'salvage', the property of anyone who could retrieve it. The wee devil could do 'onythin', so he dragged it to the surface, emptied the water out and made for Luce Bay. The tide was still out as the creature dragged it across the sand to where Michael was standing. The magician nodded his admiration.

'Juist ae mair try,' said the imp gleefully.

'Aye,' said Michael with a long, resigned sigh, 'Juist ae mair try.'

He stood looking out at the sea and the gulls as they sailed past, summer white against the blue. He looked at the broad Solway sands, then to the vessel and said, 'That's a truly magnificent boat, and it disnae need to gang back tae the bottom o the sea. We get lots of storms here and I need somethin tae keep it safe; whit I need is a rope.'

'A rope?' said the wee devil, barely concealing his surprise.

'Aye, a rope tae bind it ticht tae the land.'

'Whit kinna rope: a gress rope, a strae rope, a heather rope, a bark rope?'

'No!'

'Would ye no prefer a chain?' His tone had now turned to mockery.

'No!' said Michael, pausing as if for effect. 'I want yin makit oot o Solway saund.'

'Frae saund?' The words came almost as a screech. 'Can I no juist mak ye a saund castle?' The imp was jiggling with the giggles.

'No! Juist a rope o saund.' Michael said quietly.

'A rope o saund,' repeated the devil, driving his claws into the beach. Within minutes he had created an exquisite sand-stranded rope with a loop at either end.

Michael grinned, 'By Jove, young fella, I think ye've duin it. Three oot o three.' Michael held out his hand and shook the devil's scaly claw. The devil pulled himself up to his full three feet and grinned with pride. Michael looked past the devil and grimaced, 'Oh dear,' he said, 'I think ye had better watch oot.'

'Whit?' said the puzzled imp.

'Here comes the tide.' They both nimbly tripped up above the watermark as the incoming water quickly inundated the rope. With great patience they both waited until the tide once again receded. When it did, the rope was … GONE!

'I think ye micht need tae hae anither try,' said Michael to the obviously shocked and wide-eyed imp. The poor wee devil set to work, this time producing a work of pure beauty. 'Impressive,' said Michael, genuinely, 'but I think ye better watch oot, fer here comes the tide.'

In horror, the devil watched the tide come in and go out. Again the rope was …GONE!

The imp stood, his face held in his hands, his mouth open with disbelief. 'Hoo many goes dae ye get?' asked Michael innocently.

'Three,' wailed the imp.

'I think ye micht need some help?'

'Aye!' In a puff of foul-smelling smoke the wee devil disappeared back to Hell. He raced up to his master, 'Sir, help!'

'Whit is it?' said the mighty Lord of Hell.

'Michael Scott is beatin me.'

'If ye dinnae get back up there I'll beat ye as weel.'

'No, I mean he wants me tae mak a rope of saund an it's impossible. He's beat me twice.'

'Whit?' said the Devil in a fury, 'Michael Scott has beat me ance and he's no aboot tae beat me again. Come wi me.'

Michael was admiring his boat when, with a thunderclap announcement, Lucifer appeared beside him, the wee imp in tow. 'So, Michael Scott, ye want a rope o saund. I'll show ye a rope of saund.' With this he drove his mighty hands into the sand and in a blur began to fashion a rope. Michael now admired the terrible magnificence of this mighty creature before him: the fallen angel who had defied God. A God who could have so utterly destroyed him, yet let him live to offer a challenge to humankind. There was something profoundly ridiculous about this moment and Michael gloried in it.

When the Devil had finished he stepped back and beckoned Michael to look at the creation. 'Wow! said the man genuinely, stunned by what lay before him: The rope looked like it had been formed from silks and satins, and was encrusted in sands that took on the lustre of diamonds, rubies, emeralds and other precious and semi-precious stones. It would have outshone the very stars.

'I bow afore yer magnificence, yer Lordship. I dinnae think onybody in the universe, except, of course, the Creator himsel, cuid hae created sic a work.'

'Indeed,' said the Devil, an edge of threat in his voice. 'Noo we shall hae ane mair wee challenge afore I drag ye doon tae Hell whaur I can hae some exquisite pleesure in roastin yer insolent saul.'

'Ane thing first, Yer Majesty.'

'Aye, whit is it?'

'Dae ye like gettin yer feet wat?'

'Of coorse I dinnae like gettin ma feet wat. I come frae Hell whaur it is hot an burny.'

'Ye better watch oot then, for here comes the tide.'

Big as he was, Lucifer nimbly leapt out of the way as, once again, the tide came in.

Michael put his hands behind his back and walked about the shore, whistling as the wee imp looked nervously up at a discomforted Devil.

The tide turned and the sea slipped away. They all stood together and looked, but the rope was … GONE!

Michael gave the wee devil a wink then looked up at the Lord High Devil. 'I think ye'll find that is three oot o three, Yer Majesty.'

For a moment the Devil clawed the air and with a might roar and a clap of thunder disappeared back into the depths of Hell leaving behind the smell of sulphur and brimstone ... and the wee imp.

'Well wee man. Whit noo?' asked Michael.

'I suppose I better get back, though, I think I micht wait a wee bittie until he finds some ither body tae pick on. It will be pandaemonium doon there.' He stifled a giggle.

So the wee imp stayed and kept the magician company until, at last, Michael's family came home. And what a welcome: a brand new fishing boat and, of course, a bag of gold. Did they all live happily ever after? No, life's not like that, but they did pretty well.

The Fause Knight Upo the Road

'Oh whaur are ye gaun?'	going
Quo the fause knight upo the road;	false; upon
'I'm gaun tae the scule,'	school
Quo the wee boy, an still he stude.	stood
'Whit is that upo yer back?'	
Quo the fause knight upo the road;	
'Atweel it's ma buiks,'	books
Quo the wee boy, an still he stude.	

'Whit's that ye've got on yer airm?'
Quo the fause knight upo the road;
'Atweel it's ma peit,'   peat *(for the schoolfire)*
Quo the wee boy, an still he stude.

'Wha's aucht thae sheep?'   owns
Quo the fause knight upo the road;
'They're mine an ma mither's,'
Quo the wee boy, an still he stude.

'How mony o them are mine?'
Quo the fause knight upo the road;
'Aa they that hae blae tails,'   blue
Quo the wee boy, an still he stude.

'I wiss ye were on yon tree,'   wish; yonder
Quo the fause knight upo the road;
'An a guid ladder unner me,'
Quo the wee boy, an still he stude.

'An the ladder for tae break,'
Quo the fause knight upo the road;
'An ye fer tae faa doon,'
Quo the wee boy, an still he stude.

'I wiss ye were on yon sie,'   sea
Quo the fause knight upo the road;
'An a guid bottom unner me,'
Quo the wee boy, an still he stude.

'An the bottom fer tae break,'
Quo the fause knight upo the road;
'An ye tae be droont,'   drowned
Quo the wee boy, an still he stude.

THE BLACK SORCERER

Just over two hundred and fifty years ago, twin sisters Nan and Jean Boone lived with their mother and father near Dumfries. Twins, especially identical twins, are usually inseparable, so when the first-born girl, Jean, said, 'I want to gang oot intae the warld oan ma ain,' it came as a great surprise, especially to her twin, who was considerably upset. However, she did say that she would be back in 'twalmonth an a day', which made things better, but only a little. The girl went off on her travels but after a year and a day she had not returned and her family were, as you would expect, fearful and worried. So much so the younger twin said that she would go and find her sister. To help her on her way her mother gave her a bobbin of wool, a golden needle, a packet of pins and a silver thimble. 'Ye neer ken when ye wull hae need o them.' Her father gave her a gold coin. 'Dinnae spend it until ye hae tae.' Finally they gave her a pen-knife with their blessings and said she must write home as often as she could. So the courageous girl set off south to the Debateable Lands of the Border country. She had no problem in describing her sister, 'She luiks the spit o me.' For she was.

No one in the Debateable Lands had seen Jean, so Nan headed westwards into Galloway; still there was no sign. Not even in the lands to the north past Moniaive and Sanquhar was she to be found. On the edge of giving up hope, Nan decided at last to go east. Passing by Wanlockhead she crossed over the Lowther Hills and down in to the Glen of the Evan Water. There she passed an old gypsy man and woman with a Shetland pony pulling a rickety cart. 'Hail sister, weel met,' said the woman, 'Ye luik like a body on a mission.'

'Indeed I am,' said the Nan, 'I am in search o ma sister wha is gane this past year an mair.'

'Did she travel alane?' asked the woman.

'Aye.'

'Then aiblins the fates hae brocht ye here, for a wee bittie further on near Beattock is the castle o the Dark Sorcerer. It is said that he is fond o young lassies and taks them as his slaves. Mind ye, he's no a man tae meddle wi. Were ye tae gang there it is likely ye will end up jiggert bi ane o his cantrips.'

'Hoo exactly dae I get there?'

'Oh lass! I shouldnae hae telt ye. Ye're gaunnae go?'

'Aye!'

'I thocht that. As ye gang doon the glen ye'll see whaur it widens oot. There's a track tae yer richt. Tak that, an mind hoo ye go.'

'I wull. Thank ye baith.'

Just before Beattock, Nan turned right and headed along a rough track into the hills. As she walked, avoiding the many potholes, she passed a young cadger hauling a heavy cart overloaded with pots and pans. As he staggered past, she called to him saying, 'Young sir, why dae ye struggle wi sic a load when a pownie wuid ease yer darg.'

'Tis ma job; an besides I hae nae money tae purchase sic a thing.'

She took a shining to the young man and was eager to help him, so she put her hand in her pouch and pulled out the gold coin, 'Tak this an buy yersel a pownie.'

'I appreciate yer kindness, but I couldnae tak yer money. An besides, I dinnae ken ye.'

'Ma name is Nan, sae ye ken me noo an ye will tak it, an I'll hear nae mair aboot it. It's daein naethin in ma pootch. I cannae bear tae see anither owerburthint in life, sae tak it.'

Who was he to argue with such a forthright manner, so he conceded, 'Well, my name is Ragnald an ye hae the kindest disposition o onybody I hae eer met. I hope I can return the favour ae day.' He took a step back and looked her up and down, 'In the meantime, micht I enquire whaur ye are bound?'

'I am aff tae the castle o the Dark Sorcerer tae find ma sister Jean.'

A look of concern came over his face. 'I'm thinkin that is no a cannie thing tae dae, Nan.' He looked her straight in the eye, 'But ye will no chynge yer mind, wull ye?'

'Naw!' she said firmly.

'In that case, let me gie ye a word o advice: if ye gang, dinnae believe aa ye see nor aa ye hear.'

'I wull mind that. Thank ye.'

'Naw! Thank ye, an fare weel. I hope we meet again.'

She nodded, turned and set off purposefully down the road. 'Me tae,' she said quietly to herself as she strode out.

She had gone no more than a few hundred yards when she spied another young man among a group of wind-stunted hawthorn trees. Although an obviously able young man, his clothes were in tatters and he was attempting to fix the ripped cloth with thorns. Each time he reached up to get more thorns, the ones holding the rips together broke. It was altogether a frustrating exercise for the lad.

'Ye seem to be in a wee bit o a fankle.'

'Aye. I'm no suir gin these thorns are helpin or hindrin.'

'I think I can help ye.' Nan opened her pouch and took out the packet of pins. 'Haud still or ye'll reeve it mair.' She nimbly pinned the material together and in no time the young man's clothes looked half respectable.'

'Hoo can I thank ye?' said the young man graciously, 'Unfortunately I hae nothing to repay ye wi.'

'Yer thanks is eneuch,' said Nan. 'It's a hard warld when ye cannae help a fella traveller.'

'Indeed! An whaur are ye gaun yersel?'

'Tae the castle o the Dark Sorcerer.'

'That's no a place fer a braw lassie like yersel.'

'I thank ye kindly fer yer compliment, but I hae tae find ma sister and I jalouse that he has taen her.'

'I see ye're determint tae gang.'

'Aye!'

'In that case, let me tell ye that gowd and siller are pertection agin evil.'

'Thank ye for yer guidance, young sir. Noo I must be on ma wey. Fareweel.'

'An fareweel tae ye.'

Nan followed the track into the hills, curving upwards and to the left. As she passed a steep slope, above her was large, dark crag on which sat a great, black castle. There was little doubt that this was the lair of the Dark Sorcerer. She found her way to the massive black, oak doors and banged on the massive, black doorknocker. After a short while the door creaked open and a seemingly affable large man dressed all in black with a black, broad-brimmed hat and a black cloak stood there smiling at her. 'Can I help you?' he said kindly.

'I seek ma sister. Ye wull ken her because she is my twin and double.'

'There are many young women who work for me and many are young and bonnie like you. If you will come in and wait I will see what I can do.' The man led her to a small antechamber with two chairs on either side of a log fire. 'Please take a seat, I will be back shortly.'

Nan sat in the large ornate chair beside the fire and waited. The room was wood-panelled with two occasional tables topped with Egyptian vases. Framed papyrus covered in hieroglyphics hung on the panelled sections of the walls. Nan had never seen anything quite so beautiful and so strange. Were these magic spells? If so, what did they mean? She was so caught up in her curiosity that she did not notice the flames of the fire creeping towards her until it was nearly too late. She rose quickly from the chair and made to run for the door when the words of the young cadger came to her, 'Dinnae believe aa ye see an aa ye hear.' Though the flames licked about her and the heat was intense, she sat and suffered it. Gradually, the flames withdrew. As she studied one of the papyruses the sound of a distant cry came to her. She turned her head to hear it better and

thought that it called 'sister'. It got louder until she could clearly hear her sister's own voice calling, 'Sister come and help me. Please, please come and help me. Save me.' An almost uncontrollable urge to run to the voice began to overwhelm her but then the young man's warning came again, 'Dinnae believe aa ye see an aa ye hear.' Nan then removed the wool from her pouch and began to bind herself to the chair. This done, she put her hands over her ears to deaden the sound. Though it still got through it was more bearable. Gradually it too faded. Taking out her knife she cut herself free.

Just as she tucked the knife back in her pouch the door opened and the man returned. 'You're still here?'

'Whaur else wad I be? I wis hopin for ye tae come back wi ma sister.'

'Yes, well I think I may have found her. I'll need you to come and tell me which one she is.'

He strode out of the room before Nan could explain again their likeness. She ran after him as he stepped through a door into a courtyard. As she passed through, the door slammed hard behind her. She stopped abruptly, for before her stood twelve statues each a perfect likeness of her sister and, of course, herself. The man stopped and spun about, the black cloak billowing out behind him. His countenance took on the power of who and what he was, the Black Sorcerer. 'Before you are twelve images of your sister; one is indeed your lost twin. You have a choice: you can leave here now, unharmed, but without your sister; or you can guess which one is truly her. If you choose wrongly you will become as her and be with me forever. What is it to be?'

Nan looked along the figures, which were identical in every way. There was no way to tell them apart. Her heart kept missing beats, giving her the feeling of suffocation. Either choice was the devil's choice: that was until the words of the raggedy, young man came to her, 'Gowd an siller are pertection agin evil.' She fumbled a moment in her pouch then pulled from it the silver thimble. Placing it on her right index finger she stepped up to the first statue and touched it on the arm with the thimble. The silver turned black. She walked along the line touching each in turn until the last where the thimble turned to shining silver. In the same moment the stone turned to living flesh and there was her missing sister.

Tearfully, they threw their arms about each other until they realised that the sorcerer would be enraged, which he truly was. Grabbing Jean by the arm, Nan dragged her from the courtyard. Once through the great oak door of the castle they ran pell-mell down the hill as a mighty voice called after them, 'You think you can so easily escape. Run, but you cannot outrun my hound.' From behind, a baying was heard and briefly turning her head Nan saw a mighty black wolf-like beast bearing down on them. Spinning about, she deftly pulled the golden needle from her pouch. Standing her ground she waited until the last moment before thrusting the needle between the eyes of the dog. It exploded in a cloud of dust which melted into the air. There was a howl of rage from the castle. 'Gold and silver have served you well, but they will not protect you against me.' The sorcerer leaped from the wall, his great black cloak spreading like wings behind him. With nothing left but the pen-knife, she pulled it from the pouch and threw it with all her might. What she did not know was that the little blade was coated with her parents' blessings. The tiny weapon went straight through the black heart of the sorcerer and all that landed in front of the girls was a shower of fading dust and an empty cloak.

Jean embraced Nan. 'Ye hae muckle smeddum Nan. I'm prood o ye.'

Nan took her sister by the shoulder. 'It wisnae smeddum, Jean, it was luve.' They hugged again; at the same time the ground began to tremble. They looked above them to see the castle split apart. As battlements tumbled towards them, the sisters turned and fled down the slope, pursued by stones. Just in time, they ducked under an overhang of rock as boulders crashed over them. They wisely waited until all had settled before setting off down the hill.

As they reached the valley they passed a finely dressed young man. 'There's a familiar face,' he said. 'Or, suid I say, twa familiar faces.' He laughed at his own joke.

The lasses stopped and looked him over. Nan was sure she had seen him before. He held out his arms as if to say, 'It's me,' and grinned.

'Is it really you?' asked Nan.

The young man put his hand in his pocket and pulled the gold coin Nan had given him earlier. 'Wull this convince ye?' he asked.

Nan shook her head. 'I dinnae unnerstaun. Whit happent?'

'I an ma aulder brither Jaimie stoppit by the castle tae beg a roof fer the nicht. I dinnae ken whit happent tae him, but I wis cursit by the sorcerer and made tae travel the roads puuin that cairt. Somehoo the curse wis liftit.' He gave them a look of curiosity. 'Wis it somethin tae dae wi ye?' Nan told him all that had happened at the castle. He looked at her in amazement. 'Ye are a byordinar lassie.'

They heard the sound of hooves behind them and horses with an open carriage pulled up alongside. The young driver doffed his hat. 'Wid onybody care fer a hurl?' he said.

'Weel if it isnae ma brither in mischance,' said Ragnald. 'Hoo are ye Jaimie?'

'Grand!' said Jaimie. 'Yersel?'

'Couldnae be better,' said Ragnald. He turned to the twins, 'This is Jean an this is Nan.' His eyes lingered on the younger twin.

'I think I hae met yer brither afore,' said Nan.

'Indeed ye huv, for which I am bethankit,' said Jaimie lifting a small pouch from between his feet. 'I think these preens belang tae ye.'

Nan took the pouch. 'I'll juist haud on tae them in case they are needed again.'

'Aiblins we cuid gie these lasses a lift hame?' said Ragnald.

'It wid be ma pleesur,' said Jaimie, leaning down and offering a hand to Jean who climbed on to the seat beside him. Ragnald and Nan climbed on to the seats behind and they set off on the twenty miles to Dumfries.

In that six-hour journey, Nan and Jean discovered that the young men jointly owned a small estate on the Nith near Dalswinton and had been to Edinburgh to attend to legal matters regarding the land. Six hours was long enough for the young people to become well acquainted and in time Jean married Jaimie and the bold Nan married Ragnald and they :

Leevit happy, and deeit happy,
And neer drank oot o a dry cappy.

9

WITCHES AND WARLOCKS

In the seventeenth century, Scotland was in the grip of supernatural hysteria. Even King James VI got in on the act with his treatise on the matter, *Daemonologie*: *The fearefull aboundinge at this time in this countrie, of these detestable slaues of the Deuill, the Witches or enchaunters, hath moved me (beloued reader) to dispatch in post, this following treatise of mine, not in any wise (as I protest) to serue for a shew of my learning & ingine, but onely (mooued of conscience) to preasse / thereby, so farre as I can, to resolue the doubting harts of many; both that such assaultes of Sathan are most certainly practized, & that the instrumentes thereof, merits most severly to be punished.*

And punished severely they were: by hanging, strangling and burning. Whenever hens stopped laying, cows stopped producing milk or unusual mishaps occurred, some poor body would be accused. Sometimes feuds, old grudges or plain fear resulted in the most awful crimes being committed, mainly against women, though men were often implicated. The basis for this first tale was probably the case of Elspeth McEwan from Balmaclellan who was jailed in Kirkcudbright Tolbooth as a witch, kept in appalling conditions for two years, tortured and finally strangled and burned on Silver Craigs on the Barrhill above the town.

THE BLUE CLEW (CONVICTA ET COMBUSTA)

The old witch was taken on to the Barrhill and mounted on a pyre. The executioner asked her, 'Dae ye hae a last wish Elspeth?'

'Aye!' says she, 'Can ye gang doon tae the Tolbooth and bring me ma blue clew?'

A young runner was sent to retrieve the ball of wool and returned twenty minutes later. The executioner handed the clew to Elspeth, stepped back and lit the pyre. Smoke rose up, obscuring the unfortunate woman. In that moment she took the end of the wool in one hand and, taking the ball in the other, threw it into the sky. She then climbed the wool and disappeared.

WITCH JEAN

In the early nineteenth century, Jean Nelson lived in a hut on the Mull of Galloway. From the outside it looked ramshackle but on the inside it was homely, cosy and neatly kept. She was a kind, if solitary, soul but because of bad lumbago Jean would often be confined to her dwelling for long periods, or be seen shuffling along her track bent over. Her wrinkled, smoke-blacked face and lack of front teeth did nothing to help her appearance. Because of her unusual ways it was rumoured that Jean was a witch and when a local farmer's two cows suddenly stopped producing their usual quota of milk, Jean was blamed. To stop her putting the evil eye on his cows the farmer barricaded Jean into her hut. It was some days before she was discovered and released. Jean complained to the authorities and two arbiters were sent to investigate. They did a fine job, for they discovered that the farmer's milkmaid had many admirers and she was treating each to the farmer's milk. The case was settled in Jean's favour and she was awarded damages: four stones of oatmeal, four pounds of butter and the farmer was also ordered to deliver her peat for her fire over the next two seasons.

However, once established, the rumour persisted. And so it was that when a new minister died suddenly, eyes turned to Jean, for she had been seen walking between the minister and the other clergymen who were conducting his ordination. Had the minister given Jean a small present, all would have been well. Jean scoffed at the nonsense, but the new minister was impressed upon to deliver small gifts to Jean, and often.

Sometime later, in the early hours, a farmer noticed a hare underneath one of his cows. Shortly afterwards, his cows' milk output reduced by half. The farmer, believing, as many did, that witches often shapeshifted into the form of a hare, took out his gun and went hunting. He located the innocent animal and fired in its direction. A genuine hare would have dropped down dead; instead this beast only appeared slightly ruffled and shot off in the direction of Jean's abode. When it was heard that Jean was confined to her hut, this was proof enough that she had been the guilty party, notwithstanding her lumbago. She was called Witch Jean until her death, and afterwards.

BREAKING THE SPELL

Jenny McLean was a bonnie young lass and lived with her mother at Auchneel near Leswalt on the Rhins of Galloway. When she reached the age of fifteen she took ill and turned quite jaundiced. Her face looked more like that of a corpse than a young woman in her prime. Local rumour was that she had been put under some witch's spell, but there was no one about who might fit that description, and so hard-earned money was spent on medicines that had no effect.

One of Jenny's brothers was a bit of a rogue and inclined to pranks. He and his friends had rather cruelly decided to tie up a cat and put it down the lum (or chimney) of Auld

Sarah Corkran. An overtly religious woman, the idea was to make her think the devil was coming for her. With a punt up on to the roof from one of his pals, the boy slipped silently up the thatch and looked down the chimney. He saw Auld Sarah on her knees holding a piece of heart-shaped wax into which she was sticking pins and muttering something about Jenny that he could not make out.

The lad poured down some flowers of sulphur producing blue flames in the fireplace then dropped the cat down, instantly pulling it back up and giving the woman the fright of her life. Young McLean went straight home and told his mother of what he had seen. So concerned was she that she sent a horse to collect the local wise woman, Bella Lynn.

Bella was worried and decided serious action was needed; so at midnight she took a blue Spanish cockerel and cut its throat with a flint. She then took out its heart and stuck nine pins into it then roasted the heart on the fire. At the same time, she commanded Jenny to take the bible and read the fifth chapter of St Matthew backwards. Bella then gave Jenny the heart and made her eat it, dipping it nine times in salt. When this was done Jenny was ordered to take nine sips of water and go to bed.

Next morning Jenny rose a hale and hearty young woman. As for Auld Sarah Corkran, she took a bad leg that plagued her ever afterwards.

WHUPPITY STOORIE

In the Debateable Lands twixt Annan and England was the clachan of Kittlerumpit, and there a guidwife's not-so-guidman had disappeared. Some said he had abandoned her because of her big red nose and bloodshot eyes; some said he had been abducted by a press gang for the navy. Either way, the woman was distraught, more so for the sake of her nursing bairnie than for herself. Her only consolation was a big fat pig that she doted on as much as the child. Nothing pleased her more than to scratch the back of the sow and listen to its approving grunts. But fate was about to deal her a second blow, for only days after her man was gone the sow keeled over, legs in the air, about to breathe its last. It was the final straw: the poor woman plopped down on her knocking stone, bairnie on her knee and sobbed tears fit to flood the land – in truth, she cried more for the pig than her guidman.

Now the guidwife's cottage sat on a hill backed by a fir wood. As she sat on her knocking stone, her bairnie on her knee, vainly trying to stem the flow of her tears with her pinafore, she noticed someone coming up the hill towards her house. Though not unusual, the deportment and appearance of the figure caught her interest: she was an older-looking woman, though sure of foot to the point of being sprightly. She was dressed in green with a short, white apron, a black velvet hood and a steeple-crowned beaver hat on her head. Her walk was assisted by a stout staff, the height of herself. To the guidwife she also had elegance and grace that set her out as a lady, so much so that the guidwife automatically rose, curtsied before blurting out, 'Madam, I'm ane o the maist unfortunate woman alive.'

The woman glowered and said, 'I dinnae wish tae hear piper's news and fiddler's tales, guidwife. I ken ye've tint yer guidman – we had waur losses at the Shirramuir; an I ken yer sow is unco sick. Noo, whit will ye gie me gin I cure her?'

'Onything yer leddyship's madam likes,' said the woman, unfortunately not realising who she was dealing with.

'Let's wat thooms on that bargain,' said the woman spitting on her thumb. Thumbs were wet, the bargain sealed and the woman entered the pig's sty. She glowered at the sow and began muttering to herself something that sounded to the guidwife like:

Pitter, patter
Haly *watter*   holy

From her pouch she removed a small oil-filled bottle. She poured some of the oil on to her right hand and began to rub it over the pig's snout, behind it ears and finally on its tail. Rising from her labours she proclaimed, 'Get up beast!' Instantly the pig shot up and dashed away to its trough.

The guidwife was overjoyed and made to kiss the hem of the woman's dress but was rebuked. 'I'm no sae fond o fashions,' said the woman stepping back quickly. 'Noo that I hae richtit yer sick beast, let us end our siccer bargain. You'll no find me an unreasonable greedy body – I aye like tae dae a guid turn for a smaa reward – an aa I ask and *wull* hae, is that lad on you bosom.'

The guidwife realised suddenly who and what she was dealing with and wailed with remorse. The woman was a witchy woman or of the fairy folk. She prayed, wailed, begged and cursed but all to no avail. The fairy woman was unmoved. 'Ye spare yer din, skirlin as if I was deif as a doornail; but this I'll let ye tae wit – I cannae, *by the law we leeve on*, tak yer bairn till the third day efter this day; an no then, if ye can tell me ma richt name.' The fairy woman then disappeared round the end of the pigsty. As for the guidwife, she fell off the knocking stone in a swoon.

The poor guidwife could not sleep that night, nor the next, holding so tightly on to her child she near squeezed the breath from it. In her anxiety she decided to take a walk in the woods to try and ease her troubled mind.

In among the woods was an old quarry covered in grass in the middle of which was a spring well. As the guidwife approached she could hear the whirr of a spinning wheel and the sound of singing. Not wishing to disturb the lilt, she crept through the bushes and peered over the rim of the quarry. There before her was the green fairy working at some lint. As she worked she chanted:

| *Little kens oor* guid *dame at* hame | good, home |
| *That* Whuppity Stoorie *is my name* | Whipped Dust |

The guidwife rolled on her back in delight, suppressing the urge to scream with the pleasure of it. 'May the Deil tak her fer the begunker that she is. We'll see how she likes tae be begunkit.'

As ill-served as she had been, the guidwife was not without a sense of humour, and that side of her nature now came to the fore

as she prepared her wee joke. At the appointed time she firstly set
her bairnie by the knocking stone, dishevelled her clothes, dragged
her mutch down over one ear and set her mouth in a twist. She
then lifted her pinafore to her face and began to howl into it.
Occasionally peering over the pinnie, she saw the fairy woman
nimbly making her way up the hill. The guidwife howled louder.
The green woman stood before her and, with a voice already
sensing victory, proclaimed, 'Guidwife o Kittlerumpit. Ye weel ken
whit I hae come fer: staund and deleever!'

The guidwife wailed louder, wrung her hands and fell forward
on to her knees, 'Sweet Madam, spare ma onlie bairnie; tak ma
auld soo, but lae me ma wean.'

'The Deil tak the soo. Tis no the flesh o an aul grunt that I seek,
so dinnae be contramawcious an gie me the gett this instant.'

'If ye'll no tak the soo, tak me instead.'

The fairy laughed in scorn, 'The Deil's in ye wumman and ye are
but dementit. Wha in their richt mind wid hae taen a jad like thee?'

Though possessing two bleared eyes and a rather large ruddy
nose, the Guidwife o Kittlerumpit thought herself as fine as any
woman around and took affront at the slander. In a mighty pique
and red eyes all ablaze, she slowly rose to her feet, straightened
her mutch, brushed down her pinafore then, taking it between
both thumbs and fingers, did a mock curtsey. 'Oooh! So ye think
that I am nae fit tae tie the shoestring o her maist ryal princess,
Whuppity Stoorie.' The last two words were spat out in vengeance.
In that very instant the green woman shot in the air as if propelled
from a cannon. Landing with a crash, she threw herself downhill
and away in a screaming rage.

As for the guidwife, she laughed herself breathless. She lifted her
bairnie and held it with her deep motherly love; then turning it so
she could see its bonnie face, she crooned:

A goo an a gitty *ma bonnie wee* tyke	coochie-coo, dog
Ye'se noo hae your fower-oorie;	four-hour feed
Sin *we've gien* Auld Nick *a* bane *tae* pyke,	since, Devil, bone, pick
Wi his wheels *an his Whuppity Stoorie.*	wheels of Hell

TO SHOE A WITCH

Two bothy-lads shared a bothy at a farm near Tongland. The farm was owned and run by a woman in her middle years. She was not a bad mistress but sometimes worked the boys over-hard; so much so that once in bed they were sound asleep in moments. However, one of the lads began to lose weight and in the mornings often looked like he had been up all night. 'Ye are getting ower shilpit and forfochten,' said his friend. 'Whit is up wi ye?'

'I cannae tell,' said the lad, 'but were ye tae lie on ma bed-stock, ye wid be as shilpit as masel.'

The friend agreed to do so and lay in his friend's bed. In the middle of the night he was woken by his mistress placing a bridle over his head. 'Up horsie,' she commanded. In that second he turned into a fine grey stallion. The mistress leaped on his back and with a prompt from her spurs he took off like the wind. Rivers, lochs, forests and mountains sped by as he effortlessly galloped on. On a wooded hill she pulled hard on the reins, dismounted and led him into the trees where other horses had been tethered. Tying the bridle to a branch, she walked off up the slope. Shortly afterwards the hilltop began to glow from a great fire and the sound of revelry, screams, laughter and mirth.

The bothy-boy realised he was at a witches' Sabbat. In the light of the fire he could see the other horses around him and, though in a different guise, he could make out other bothy-boys he knew. With great effort he began to pull at the bridle and by twisting his head managed to ease it from his head. He untied it from the tree and then hid in a bush. In time, his mistress returned and began to search for her mount. The boy leaped from the bush and quickly put the bridle about her head. 'Up horsie,' he said, and she instantly turned to great black mare. He leaped on her back and urged her forward. She likewise sped off effortlessly on the road home. However, rather than go back to the farm, the lad headed to his uncle's house. Though early, he roused the man, who was a blacksmith, saying that he had an urgent job for his mistress to shoe this unshod mare. In no time the uncle had the horse shod and the boy set off for home.

He rode up to the farmhouse, dismounted and removed the bridle. It was still dark so he slipped back into the bothy for an hour's sleep, hiding the bridle under a loose stone in the eaves. At first light he went back to the farmhouse and entered. There in the kitchen was his mistress pathetically attempting to remove horseshoes from her hands and feet. Taking pity, he gently undid the nails and treated the wounds, but not before obtaining her guarantee that she would cease her diablerie and ease up on the lads' workload. She agreed after being reminded that he still had the bridle.

THE KIRKCOWAN WITCH

In the wee village of Kirkcowan to the west of Wigtown lived a woman called Nanny McMillan. Though she lived close by the manse, she was considered more inclined to Auld Nick, and people tended to stay clear of her. If they did inadvertently come into contact with her, they treated her with deference and respect.

In the village there also lived a hunter who specialised in hares. Long experience had turned him into a crack shot, insisting that it was cruel to wound an animal and leave it in distress. On the rare times he did it himself he would track the animal through stream, bog and gorse to put it out of its misery. His particular favourite hunting ground was the glebe that ran from the manse down to the River Tarff. The area was dotted with clumps of gorse and broom, ideal for hares to hide away in.

There was one particular hare of a mixed colouring who always somehow managed to avoid his bullets. Assuming there was more than just luck involved, he loaded a silver bullet into the gun. On seeing the hare he took his time, to be certain of his shot before pulling the trigger. He shot and the hare rolled head over heels into the gorse bushes. The hunter had enough time to see that there was blood on the head of the hare before it seemed to recover and make for the village. He ran after it and just managed to see it run round the back of Nanny McMillan's cottage. He followed but lost the track at the back of the house. He noticed Nanny's door was

slightly ajar so summoned up courage and knocked on it. There was no answer so he knocked again, this time louder. 'Haud oan a meenit,' came an agitated voice from inside. The door opened slightly, 'Whit dae ye want?'

'Hae ye seen a parti-colourit mauken gaun by yer door?' the hunter enquired.

'I hae seen nowt,' came the voice.

'Are ye shuir?' he said, pressing on the door in his eagerness. The door slid open and the man leaped back when he saw Nanny with a bloody bandage just above her eye. The exact place he had shot the hare.

THE MINISTER'S WIFE

In the days before elastic, men and women employed the use of a garter with which to tie up their stockings. This was usually above the knee, though occasionally on the narrow part of the leg just below the knee. Here is how a garter revealed a rather unusual witch.

In the small town of Whithorn lived a tailor who was also an elder of the church, that is, a member of the public who is ordained to take on some of the duties of the minister. The tailor, as the times required, was often 'whipping the cat', in other words, travelling round the countryside plying his trade. Many people of the time spun their own yarn and often did their own weaving. The tailor would visit a house or farm, measure up the person requiring the garment, and cut and sew the material there and then before moving on to the next settlement.

On this particular occasion, a Wednesday in autumn, the tailor had been invited to make Sunday suits for a farmer and his two sons; the tailor took his guidwife as a travelling companion. Late on the road home, they had just passed a 'rotten row', a rat-infested row of cottages, when they came upon an old grain-drying kiln whose great chimney had partially collapsed. The adjoining grain room was still thatched and had a rough-planked door from which light streamed out through the gaps. Out of an overwhelming curiosity, the garment maker and his wife tiptoed up to the web-covered window and peered in. There they saw and heard a group of women gathered round a large open book engaged in strange incantations. The one nearest was leaning over the table so that her dress had lifted, revealing a length of stocking and a bright purple garter just below the knee. The tailor felt his wife grip him hard on the arm. She moved close and whispered, 'They're witches. It's yin o they witches' covens.'

'Aye,' whispered he, 'an that's the meenister's wife hingin ower the table.'

'Sae it is!' the wife whispered in shock.

Unable to bear this unholy sight further, and in fear for their immortal souls, they tiptoed away. Later they resolved that the matter should be taken up with the kirk session on the following Sunday.

While their wives chatted in the church, the elders held the kirk session in the vestry. This included the minister and six other elders besides the tailor. He waited until 'any other business' was asked for before raising the issue. 'There is a wee maiter I wid like tae bring tae the attention o the session, and it is this.' The tailor then went on reveal the happenings of the previous Wednesday, without mentioning the purple garter.

'This is monstrous,' protested the minister. 'Ma wife wis at hame wi me.'

'Deed she wis not sir; an I can prove it, should ye be sae kind as tae gang an bid her, the session clerk's wife an ma wife tae jyne us.'

'Whit's it got tae dae wi ma wife?' blurted out the clerk.

'Nothin at aa,' said the tailor, 'I juist need her as an independent witness.'

The red-faced minister went into the church and called his wife, the clerk's wife and the tailor's wife to join the meeting.

The tailor then repeated the charge. 'Is this no sae, Phemie?'

'Aye, tis true.'

The minister's wife blazed with anger. 'Ye are quite mistaken. It must hae been some ither body. I wis at hame wi ma husband.'

'No, it wis ye,' said the tailor firmly, 'and I can prove it. Show us yer garters.'

'How daur ye,' screamed the woman.

'I daur because ma wife an I ken they are purple. We saw them as ye leaned ower that unhaly buik ye had.'

The woman blanched. 'I will no embarrass masel by liftin ma petticoats; an ye are a rogue tae suggest sic a thing.'

'I hae nae desire tae see yer petticoats,' said the tailor, 'but ye widnae object tae showin them tae the session clerk's wife, wuid ye?'

The clerk's wife, a doughty woman, in a flash lifted the minister's wife's skirt, revealing the purple satin garter. The minister's wife howled and hit out; the clerk's wife nimbly sidestepped the attack.

'I am no prepared tae tak ony mair o these wytins.' With this she turned and sped out of the building. The flustered minister made his apologies and set out after his wife.

That was the last anyone saw of the couple, for by the next Sunday they were 'ower the Border an awa'.

Now if you wish to try your own magic spells, here are a couple to consider: the first is for a boy to charm a girl and the second for a girl to charm a boy. Good luck with them.

In the pingle *or the pan,*	long-handled shallow pan
the haurnpan *o' man,*	skull
Boil the heart's-bluid o' the tade,	blood of the toad
Wi' the tallow *o' the* gled:	grease, buzzard or kite
Haweket *kail an' hen-dirt,*	hacked
Chow'd *cheese an* chicken-wort,	chewed, chickweed
Yalla puddocks champit *sma',*	yellow frogs, mashed
Spiders ten and gellocks *twa,*	earwig
Sclaters *twa, frae* foggy dykes,	woodlice, mossy walls
Bumbees *twunty, frae their* bykes,	bumblebees, hives
Asks *frae stinking* lochens *blue,*	newts, ponds
Ay, will make a better stue;	stew
Bachelors maun hae *a charm,*	may have
Hearts they hae fu' *o' harm.*	have, full
Aye the aulder, *aye the* calder,	older, colder
And the calder aye the balder.	bolder
Taps *snaw white and tails green*	tops
Snappin' *maidens o' fifteen*	smart
Mingle, mingle, in the pingle	
Join the cantrip *with a* jingle.	spell, song
Now we see, now we see	
Plots o' pauchin' *yin, twa, three.'*	boil skilfully

Or alternatively:

Yirbs *for the* blinking *queen,*	herbs, bewitching
Seeth *now, when it is* e'en,	scythe, evening
Boortree *branches, yellow* gowans,	elderberry, daisies
Berry rasps and berry rowans;	mountain ash
Deil's milk frae thrissles *saft,*	thistles
Clover blades frae aff the craft;	croft
Binwud *leaves and blinmen's* baws,	(bindwood) ivy, puffball

Heather bells and wither'd haws;
Something sweet, something soor,   sour
Time about wi mild and dour;   severe
Hinnie-suckles, bluidy-fingers,   honeysuckle, foxglove
Napple *roots and nettle stingers,*   vetch
Bags o' bees and gall in bladders,
Gowks' spittles, pizion *adders:*   cuckoospit, poison
May dew and fumarts' *tears,*   polecat
Nool *shearings,* nowt's neers,   sheep, ox kidney
Mix, mix, six and six,
And the auld *maid's* cantrip *fix.*   old, spell

10

HEATHER ALE

Niall Noigiallach, Niall of the Nine Hostages (because he held hostage a son of each of the under-kings of Ireland to ensure their loyalty), was a man of need and a man of greed, and what he wanted he got. At a banquet in his royal hall of Tara he first tasted heather ale, and he liked it. The ale had come from a passing trader and so its origin was unknown. This being so, Niall Noigiallach offered a large bag of gold to anyone who could supply him with the recipe. Such a fee could set a man or woman up for life. The word soon spread until it was heard by a man from An t-Sròn Reamhar (Stranraer), across the North Channel in Galloway. He was known locally as Sionnach, the Fox, because of his sly and cunning ways.

On hearing of the reward, Sionnach took the first boat to Ireland and went straight to Tara where he gained an audience with the High King. 'Sire,' he said, grovelling on his knees, 'I do not have the recipe you desire, but I know where it can be obtained.' He smiled ingratiatingly, then added, 'If not a bag of gold, then perhaps half a bag?' His vulpine grin showed reason for his epithet.

Niall Noigiallach's eyes narrowed. 'Perhaps. Who has the recipe?'

'Across the North Channel in my home among the Gallwesi are an ancient people who lived on the land before we came. They are those whom the Romans called the Pictii, the painted people. They are very small but have feet so large that when it rains they are said to lie on their backs and shelter under them.' The assembled courtiers burst into laughter and Sionnach looked round, pleased with himself that he had amused the throng. The stamp of the High King's boot upon the boarded floor instantly wiped away the smiles.

'If they are so small, why have you not gone and taken the recipe from them?'

'They are mighty warriors.'

'Ah!' The king nodded understandingly, 'How many of them are there?'

'A father and two sons.'

Noigiallach's eyes widened, then he burst into laughter; a hesitant moment later the crowd joined in. The Fox shrank back. 'But … but Your Majesty, you don't understand. An army of a hundred men could not defeat them.'

The king leaned forward in his chair, his demeanour all menace. 'I understand all I need to understand. So understand this Gallwesi: perhaps a hundred of your pathetic people cannot conquer them, but my warriors are the descendants of Cuchullain and of Fionn MacCumhaill. Any ten of them would be a match for all your Picts and Gallwegians.' Niall Noigiallach sat back on his throne, full of pride at being the all-powerful king of the mightiest fighting force in Gaeldom. 'But I am in a conciliatory mood and I will give you one hundred of these fine warriors to help you on your quest.'

'I … I …' the Fox was about to protest, but was waved away in dismissal by the king, who stood up and strode from the hall.

Before he knew it, the Fox was on a birlinn rowing its way with two other vessels across the North Channel. They beached at Port Logan where the warriors leaped over the side and dragged the boats above the high-water line. They then followed the Fox down the Rhinns of Galloway to the Mull across which the Picts had erected a defensive turf and stone dyke with a two-metre deep ditch on the outside. From the bottom of the ditch the climb was six metres high. At either end were vertical cliffs. Behind the dyke stood the impressive circular structure known as a broch: the building alone was near impossible to breach, even without the wall. As they approached, three heads appeared above the parapet. 'Can we help you?' called the father.

'We have come on an errand from Niall Noigiallach, High King of all Ireland,' called out Sionnach.

The Pict pursed his lips and looked at his two sons, then turned back to the Fox. 'Impressive. We are honoured. But pray tell me, what would the High King of all Ireland want with a scurrilous rogue as yourself, Sionnach?'

'You can insult me all you wish, but even you can see by the quality of men and arms I have with me that I mean business.'

The Picts nodded to each other. 'Mmm, yes, he does look like he means business,' said the father.

'Yes indeed, I would say so,' said the elder son.

'Aye. I don't think there's any doubt about that,' said the younger.

'So, what's your business, Sionnach?'

'We have to come to ask for the recipe for your heather ale.'

The father turned to his sons again. 'Did you hear that, my boys? The recipe, he wants the recipe.' He turned back to the Fox.

'And here was us thinking when we saw you arriving up all bristling with arms that you just wanted a wee drink; fighting being such thirsty work. Well, as there are only three of us and a hundred of you – I would say a hundred and one, but you're such a big fearty, Sionnach, you don't count – the answer has to be ... NO! Now bugger off back to Ireland; we have work to do.' The three heads disappeared.

Sionnach stood for a moment looking about himself, embarrassed by the failure of his bravado. He walked to the wall and shouted up. 'There's half a bag of gold in it for you.'

'Who gets the other half?' came a voice from over the wall. 'Let ... me ... guess! A wee snivelling runt of a man that has the temerity to insult one of nature's beautiful beasts. I would call you Rat but I'm short on compliments at the moment. So bugger off, the answer is still NO!'

'This is your last chance. Take the offer or we come and—'

Before he could finish, a thin stream of yellow liquid sailed over the wall and on to Sionnach's head. 'There's a *wee* sample we made earlier. It has quite a pleasant bouquet, don't you think? It has my father's seal of approval; in fact, he's just this minute passed it.' Raucous laughter rolled over the wall; even the Irishmen began to snigger.

Outraged, the Fox turned on the Dalriadans. 'You think that's funny. You go back to Ireland without the recipe and see if Niall Noigiallach is equally amused.' The laughter stopped abruptly. 'Get on with the job you were supposed to do!' he roared. Instantly three ran for the ditch, leaped in and turned their backs to the wall, another three followed and, with a help from the first three, were hoisted on to their shoulders. Another three followed, then another three until they had reached the top of the wall at which precise moment the three Picts leaped in the air and delivered a blow with a cudgel, sending all three to the bottom of the ditch; the boulders that followed made short work of the rest. Bruised and bloodied, the Irishmen retreated a safe distance.

After a brief conference they decided to attack the wall at ten different points – three Picts could not defend against that kind of relentless attack. Battle ensued and the Dalriadans hit the wall simultaneously at ten points. As they reached the top, six were dispensed with in short order but four made it over the wall. The rampart was only three feet wide so they could only advance on the Picts one at a time. Armoured in studded leather, a targe to the fore and finely sharpened sword, the Irishmen looked on these diminutive men with incredulous amusement: tiny in stature – just over a metre high – and, indeed, large-footed, each was dressed in a philamohr, a short-skirted wrap-around single piece of cloth; their bodies were covered almost entirely in tattoos and each held a club almost as big as themselves. The Irishmen laughed at what they thought was a comical sight. When the Picts threw down their clubs and held up their fists they roared with mirth. The comedy was short lived as the Picts, powered by their heavily muscled feet, ran at them. In a flash the two sons leaped in the air, kicking a Dalriadan over the wall as they passed. Another was similarly dispatched and the last was kicked so hard he disappeared over the western cliff: some say he was kicked so hard he flew all the way home to Ireland. There was nothing for it now but to make a full retreat back across the North Channel.

The fury of Niall Noigiallach was frightening to behold and the shamed warriors cowered before the High King. 'Even if it takes a thousand men, I will show these creatures real power.' And so it was that with fifty ships and nearer to fifteen hundred battle-hardened warriors, Niall Noigiallach set sail for Galloway. As before, they beached at Port Logan and marched south to the Mull of Galloway. They set up camp a hundred metres from the wall, then shortly afterwards the High King, in full battledress, stepped out and addressed the Picts. 'Hail last of the great race of the Pictii. We came to pay you great honour and respect by assembling the greatest of the warriors of Erin before you. I would give a hundred bags of gold to have but one of you as my personal guard and a thousand bags for the three of you.'

'We are not for sale, Great King,' said the father. 'We are indeed the last of our race, and it is our duty to preserve all that entails, and that includes the secret of Fraoch, the heather ale.'

'Ah yes, straight to the crux of the matter,' said the king. For a moment he looked to the ground thoughtfully and kicked away a stone. 'It would sadden my soul to see all you have created destroyed and for you to be enslaved. For you know that is what I will do, no matter how many warriors I have to call on. I have the whole of Erin at my disposal and a certain reputation to maintain. You know also that, in time, I will obtain what I want, either by persuasion ...' he paused briefly, 'or by other means.' He calmly raised his head and looked unblinkingly at the Picts, the threat made plain in his eyes.

'We shall retire to consider your words, Niall Noigiallach,' said the father. The three heads disappeared.

The king turned about and started back to his tent. 'I think that went well,' he said to no one in particular.

The Picts sat round the fire in the broch, each deep in thought about the line of their ancestors, each of whom could recite their geneaology for a thousand years. After a long time the father spoke, 'I suppose we only have one option.'

'I think so Father,' said the eldest nodding.

They both looked to the youngest. He nodded and looked hard at his father and brother, 'Aye!' he said, pulling his dirk from his belt and stabbing them both through the heart.

In the half-light of the short summer night, the young Pict left the broch, went by a secret path along the western cliffs and found his way to Niall Noigiallach's tent. The guard, taken aback by the sight of the Pict, pointed his spear at him but stepped back in alarm. The Pict looked up at him, 'I wish to see your king.'

Before the soldier could say anything, the king called out 'Let him in!' As the young man entered the king stood up, 'Welcome!' he said. 'I was, however, expecting your father. No matter; I am sure you have come to speak for them all.'

'I have come to speak for myself,' said the young man, 'for I am the last of the Picts. My father and brother are dead and the secret is mine alone. I therefore claim a bag of gold in exchange.'

'You have killed both father and brother,' said Niall. 'You are a man as ruthless as myself.'

'Perhaps,' said the Pict.

The king pointed to the druid sitting beside him. 'This man here will memorise the recipe if you will now give it to him.'

'With respect, Mighty King, I cannot give it to someone who is not my countryman. I will only give it to Sionnach. Tell him to meet me at the end of the Picts' dyke by the western cliffs and be sure he has the bag of gold. I will see him there at dawn. First, I need to go and send the souls of my kin to the Otherworld. At the least, they deserve that.'

'Indeed,' said the king.

The Pict returned home by the cliff path. He dragged timbers from outside the broch to the cliffs and built a funeral pyre. He then carried the bodies of his father and brother and laid them side by side on top. With steel and flint he fired dry moss and set the pyre alight. As it burned, he chanted an ancient lay, so full of loss and sorrow that even Niall Noigiallach wiped his eyes, complaining of sand on the wind.

As dawn split earth from sky, the Pict appeared on the cliff. Fifteen hundred warriors gathered about their king as he escorted the Fox, who carried a large bag of gold in his hand. Showing respect, the king kept his distance and urged Sionnach forward. The Gallwesi pulled back his shoulders and strode forward, a grin of pride on his face. The young man stood looking out to the western ocean. Though small in stature he was a giant presence that unnerved the traitor. Even when Sionnach stood beside him and held out the bag of gold, the Pict continued to gaze seaward. He then turned and quietly said something to the Fox.

'What did you say?' said Sionnach.

'I have just told you the recipe and you did not listen. Come closer.' Sionnach leaned closer. 'Closer,' said the Pict; the Fox bent even closer. The young man gripped his arm and leaned towards Sionnach's left ear. He then shouted with all his might so that even the horde of Irishmen heard, 'The secret is safe!' and with a mighty pull dragged them both over the cliff. The scream of the Fox blotted out the rush of the sea and the wild call of the seabirds. The sky rained gold.

Grim-faced, Niall Noigiallach looked down on the broken bodies on the rocks far below, the sea beginning to pull their shattered limbs into the deep. He turned and looked at the throng of his warrior band. 'I have just learned a great lesson in honour and loyalty. If any of you have not learned that lesson this very day, then leave, for you are no warrior of mine.' He then marched away northwards towards his ship. They all followed.

11

SONGS OF THE SOLWAY

The Solway Firth marks the western border between Scotland and England. The name is recorded in 1218 as Sulewad and denotes the ancient ford at the mouth of the River Esk. *Wad* is from the Norse, *vað*, meaning ford. *Sule* is possibly from *sule*, a pillar and may reference the Clochmabenstane, a nearby eight-foot megalith that was part of a stone circle five thousand years old. What seems most likely is that it is from *sulr* meaning *muddy*. *Firth* is Scandinavian and is cognate with the word *fiord*. The Solway Firth was, in days past, the highway to Dumfries and Galloway and was generally alive with ships trading with nearby Cumbria and the world. The Solway appears in many of the regions tales. The coastline comprises salt and mud flats or merse, impressive cliffs, shingle shores and sandy beaches where, as is the case of much of the coastline, the tide goes out for over half a mile (one kilometre). Inevitably, there are mythical creatures associated with the firth, the most famous being our mermaids, of which there are a number of tales, some herein.

Smuggling was a major industry in Dumfries and Galloway, with brandy, wine, tobacco, tea, silk and even salt being illicitly brought into the region. Sir Walter Scott, who used the infamous Solway smuggler, Captain Yawkins, as the model for Dirk Hatteraick in Guy Mannering, said, 'Few people take more enthusiastically to the *free-trade* than the men of the Solway Coast.' He might have well added, 'the women, too'.

I

Jouk the Guager

In 1777, near Ruthwell a notorious smuggler had returned from the Isle of Man. An exciseman and a constable went to the house and found a substantial amount of tobacco. As they prepared to carry it away, they were pounced on by a gang of women who made off with the contraband. The exciseman, who had been locked in the smuggler's house, escaped and made his way back to headquarters. He was given short shrift and sent back to reclaim the goods. He returned with ten men but only managed to find one bundle of tobacco in a ditch, but not before being assaulted by an army of women bearing clubs and pitchforks. Some were arrested and went to court but were acquitted, as the witnesses for the prosecution pretended to 'entertain malice against the prisoners'.

II

At Cummertrees, the excisemen raided a farmhouse in search of contraband. As they searched the house they discovered an entrance to a cellar. At this point, the farmer removed himself from the house and ran into his wife. In alarm he told of the unfolding events. 'Neer mind, they's get naethin there; it's safe.' The alert wife had seen the revenue men arrive and slipped out the back door. She then went to the cellar's outside entrance, shipped out the goods and hid them in among the whin bushes at the back of the farmstead.

III

One of Yawkins' most adventurous escapades happened in the 1780s after he had delivered a valuable cargo of spirits to Manxman's Bay near Kirkcudbright. Two revenue cutters, *The Pygmy* and *The Dwarf*, entered the Dee Estuary. One had come from the West by the Isles of Fleet and the other from the east round Raeberry Point. On sighting the cutters, Yawkins made a run for it, sailing right past the ships. So close the cutters were that he was able to throw his hat on to the deck of one and his wig on to the deck of the other. He then 'cocked a snook' at the excisemen by hoisting a barrel on to his maintop.

IV

Scotland's most famous son, Robert Burns, was himself a guager or exciseman and was involved in the apprehension of a smuggling vessel:

We'll make our maut, *and we'll brew our drink*   malt
laugh, sing, and rejoice man,
And mony *braw thanks to the* meikle *black deil,*   many, big
That danced awa wi the Exciseman.   Tax Revenue collector
The deil's awa, the deil's awa,
The deil's awa wi the Exciseman,
He's danced awa, he's danced awa,
He's danced awa wi the Exciseman.

V

THE MERMAID OF URR

To the west of Dalbeattie, the Valley of the Birches, the Dalbeattie Burn runs in to the Water of Urr. The word Urr is almost certainly the pre-Celtic word for river, and since those pre-Celtic times a mermaid would swim from the Solway up the River Urr and sit on a large, round, granite rock where the Dalbeattie Burn and the Urr meet. She was ancient, even in the ancient times, and had great wisdom, which she would share with the People of the Land. If crops failed she would have a remedy, if an animal was sick she would know the herbs that would cure it, and if a lass wanted the heart of a young man she had just the right remedy for that too. Her other great joy was to sing the ancient lays of her people: songs as old as Adam.

One young man, whose father farmed the land by the Urr, especially loved the mermaid. He would sneak along the riverbank and lie in the long grass listening to her bewitching melodies. His love was untainted by sexual desire and such a thought never crossed his mind, for he loved a pretty lass from a farm at Haugh of Urr. In time he asked her to marry him. She consented and they set up home on a farm cottage near the confluence; that way he could also hear his beloved mermaid.

His wife was happy to be married to the young farm lad but not entirely happy with his affections for the mermaid, though she never expressed her disapproval. Sadly, the young man's father died and he took control of the farm. His grief was mitigated by the news that he would soon become a father. They now moved to the more spacious farmhouse. This pleased the wife, especially as she could no longer hear the mermaid's song. The child was born and all were delighted that there was an heir to the farm. However, the child proved fractious and would not settle. All attempts were made to quiet the child, until the young farmer had the idea of taking his son to the river to hear the mermaid's refrains; in moments the child was asleep. Nightly, the father took his sojourns and nightly his wife's jealous ire rose to a fury.

It was market day in Castle Douglas and the farmer, with a few of his retainers, drove the beasts to the mart. Knowing he would be back late, the young wife called the remaining workers into the steading and ordered them to gather up their sledgehammers and go with her to the river. As the child was asleep and only a few hundred yards away, she decided to let it be. Once at the river, she ordered the men to smash the stone. 'Beggin yer pardon mistress,' said one of the men, 'but that widnae be wise, fer the marmaid is an unyirthly craitur and micht lay a glamourie aboot us aa.'

The young woman was irked at being spoken back to. 'A glamourie, ye say? Ye hae a choice: ye either risk her glamourie or the certainty o haen nae darg and yer family pit tae the road. Whit's it tae be?'

With heavy and fearful hearts the men set about reducing the rock to rubble. The young woman stayed to make sure the job was done properly then dismissed the men. She stood a short while relishing her victory. As she did so, the mermaid appeared from beneath the water. On seeing her beloved boulder was now destroyed she let out a scream that echoed off Craignair. With a self satisfied smile, the farmer's wife turned about and strode off home. As she did so the ground shuddered as if a wave had passed through the land. This was followed by an eldritch growl,

'Ye may think oan yer cot,
I'll think oan ma stane
But there'll neer be an heir
Tae this fermtoun again.'

The young woman turned briefly and gave a scornful laugh. In an instant her confidence disappeared, and in a panic she ran for home. On entering the nursery, she found the cot upturned and her son smothered beneath the bedclothes.

MAY AND THE MERMAID

Herbs have probably been used to treat ailments since the dawn of time and herbalists were greatly revered for their skill and knowledge. The exception was during the sixteenth and seventeenth centuries when the art was seen as the work of the Devil and purveyors were hounded, tortured or burned as witches or warlocks. In 1563, the Scottish Parliament passed the Witchcraft Act, sometimes referred to as the Herbalist Act. It was a brave soul that plied their trade openly, but one such fellow lived in Galloway, a place infamous for the burning of witches. What made his skill all the more dangerous to him was that he obtained it from a mermaid.

The lad, Thomas Telfer from Ferrytown of Cree, spent much of his early years in the company of his grandmother. She was from a long line of people who knew the benefits of local plants and herbs. In time, he gained his grandmother's knowledge. As doctors were few, and too expensive for common folk, Thomas was called on by neighbours and friends to assist with their ailments. For many he found a cure, or, at the worst, provided some relief.

Tom, as he was usually called, was also in love with a lass named May Goudie from Carsluith. He was never happier than when he was with May throwing skifters on the sea or lying among the heather on Cairnharrow. He was beside himself with happiness when she agreed to marry him. It was on the day of their engagement that she first spat blood. Soon her body was being ravaged and consumed and gradually she faded to a shadow. Try as he might with everything he could think of, May declined. In anguish he took himself to the shore to watch the evening sun descend in the west; its beauty did nothing to ease his pain. Helplessly he turned to go when a ripple on the placid water caught his attention. As he focused on the disturbance, a head trailing a stream of golden hair broke the surface. The heart-shaped face was more beautiful than any he had seen; her green eyes held him in thrall.

> *'Why fret ye by the shore Tom, why fret ye by the tide*
> *When bonnie May has need o ye at her ain bedside?*
> *Wuid ye let yer lover* dee *Tom when, by yer very*   die,
>   haund,   hand
> *Ye may gether wild* Muggart *that grows upon*   mugwort plant
>   *the land?'*

In fascination he watched and listened as her words bored into his soul. He staggered back and gathered his senses just in time to see the mermaid disappear beneath the waves. Thomas set out to gather mugwort. From it he made a potion and administered it to his beloved May. In no time, her colour returned and in a few weeks she was quite cured.

Thomas now became famous, and all the more because, since the mermaid sang to him, he discovered his power to find just the right herbs had magically increased. Consequently, he was now more in danger from the Church and the Witchcraft Act, which demanded the death penalty. However, having since cured Lord Ronald of Galloway of gout he was now a well-protected man. Thomas and May were married and lived long and healthy lives.

THE MERMAID OF GALLOWAY

Young William, Laird of Cowiehill, was busy preparing for his wedding to the lovely Mary which was to be the following day. The day had been long and hard, so to clear his head he invited one of his young retainers to ride out with him along the seashore. As they rode through the wood down to the sea, William was in high spirits and laughed and joked with his companion. All around, birds sang as if joining in the celebrations. William suddenly stopped his chatter upon hearing a melodic voice. He reined in his horse, as did the young retainer. Birds ceased to sing, the trees hushed and the world seemed to stop and listen to the singing that appeared to come from everywhere. William turned his head hither and thither trying to ascertain where it came from. Both men were perplexed, looking at each other with furrowed brows. 'Neer hae I heard sic a sweet sang,' said the laird in a whisper. ''Tis the voice o an angel an t'would wile the lark frae the sky as it wiles me.'

'Hae caution sir, I fear the singer an the sang,' urged the retainer, 'fer this last nicht I dreamit that ye kissit lips drippin wae bluid.' He leaned over to take his master's bridle and lead him home. 'Beware!'

William laughed, 'That's it. Haud ma steed whilst I kiss the lips that sing sae sweetly.'

'Nae maister! Dinnae kiss they lips, nor the cheek nor the hand o the sangstress if ye wish tae reach hame an mairry yer betrothit.'

William, caught in the magic of the singing, leaped from his horse and ran through the darkening woods to the beach. On a rock, washed by the incoming tide, sat the most beautiful creature William had ever set eyes on: a woman of the sea. She smiled at him as she groomed her hair of burning gold with a comb of pearl. 'A streenge restin place fer a fair maid on a rock washed by sea foam aneath a sillert muin,' he said, 'Allou me tae comb yer gowden tresses awa frae yer een sae blue.' He ran through the deepening water and leaped on to the rock beside her.

'You may comb my hair of gold, but first you must take off your doublet, for it would harm my fair skin.' William tore off the garment. 'Now you may comb my golden hair and dry it beneath the silver moon, then you may kiss my cheek.'

William, overwhelmed with ecstasy, leaned over and kissed her cheek. In that moment it was as if the waves of the sea were pleasure and were flowing over and through him and all thoughts of his betrothed faded to nothing, 'Came wi me tae ma hame an be ma luve and dine on the finest sweetmeats and drink wine as deep as yer bluid-reid lips. Lea the cauld waves fer the warmth o ma luesome airms.'

The woman of the sea smiled a knowing smile and then asked, with seeming innocence, 'But what of your betrothed who waits in her wedding dress? What will she say of the kisses that were for her and now given to me?'

William threw off the enchantment and, in remorse, cried, 'I maun awa, for the morn's morn I am tae be wed.' He leaped from the rock and waded thigh-deep through the surf. Then gripped by aching loss, he turned. 'Afore I gang, gie me a token o oor luve that I mey keep fer aye.' He waded back to the rock. In silence the mermaid pulled a strand of her long, golden hair and wrapped it in a circlet about William's head. 'Tie it no sae tichtly ma luve. It burns intil ma brain.' She said nothing, but tied it in nine witch-knots and set in it a sea pink. William tried to remove it but could not. He struggled to tear it from his head but to no avail and overpowered by her glamourie he fell in a trance at the mermaid's feet. Pitilessly she pulled his ring of betrothal from his finger and threw it along with his doublet into the waves. 'Now you are mine,' she said, exultantly.

In her tower on a primrose bank, a lass waited in vain for a lover who would never return. Endlessly she listened for his footfall but all she could hear was the song of the woodlark in the hawthorn tree, saying:

'Tak the luvelocks frae thy hair,
Let them tumble, let them fall,
Your luve nou has anither luve,
The sea-witch has him in her thrall.'

That night, Mary took a slice of her wedding cake and placed it beneath her pillow and dreamed unsettling dreams. At the eerie hour of midnight she was woken by the tinkle of a bell and felt a bone cold face press against her cheek and a hand, cold as death, touched hers. Then she saw her love and lamented:

'Oh! William, yer face is paulie	pale
Yer haunds as cauld as the winter sie	sea
Yer chafts *sae* thrawn *that aye wert* brawlie	cheeks, twisted, handsome
An yer hair is wat *with* sautie-bree.'	wet, salt water

His voice came faint and distant:

'Find anither luve sweet Mary,	
Turn yer mind awa fra me	
I am lost to ye fer aye	
Fer ma bride is nou the deep saut *sea.'*	salt

She listened again for his voice but all she could hear was the thin, cold wind from the Solway, the constant hush of waves on the shore and a distant laughter like falling crystals of ice.

THE HAUNTED SHIPS

Eight hundred years ago, on the west side of the River Nith near the estuary with the Solway Firth, Dervorguilla (Dearbhfhorghaill) built a monumental edifice in memory of her husband, John Baliol. She called it Dulce Coeur, Sweetheart Abbey. Five hundred years later, Sandy McHarg built a more humble structure just outside New Abbey, as the settlement around Dervorguilla's edifice was called: a small two-roomed thatched cottage on his modest twenty-five acres of land. This young laird was twenty-five years of age, well muscled, handsome and single. As far as he was concerned, he was likely to stay that way, happy with his lot. He had two cows, half a dozen goats, chickens, ducks and a strong reliable horse to both ride and work the plough. Considered a good catch by the lasses of the district, many found themselves just passing as Sandy worked his land. Sandy would smile politely, doff his bonnet and get on with his work.

Some five miles to the south west is Arbigland, and there dwelt a lass by the name of Janet. Comely in every way, Janet was self-sufficient and took no interest in the overtures of the young local lads. One day, requiring more pins for dressmaking, her mother sent her to Dumfries to buy some. On the road she happened to pass Sandy's smallholding just as he was rebuilding a partially fallen dry-stone dyke. Out of habit Sandy briefly raised his bonnet. At the same time Janet respectfully did a brief curtsey. In those brief glances that each gave the other they fell in love. Before he knew it he was on the road to Dumfries with her and a month later they were married.

Both being industrious, they prospered and so began a family. Soon they had a girl and a boy who thrived in the loving household.

One night, when they had settled down the two children, Sandy prepared to go out fishing.

The Solway has a unique form of fishing called haaf-netting where the fisher has an oblong net four feet deep and eighteen feet wide. Top and bottom are two eighteen feet poles with two four feet poles at either end. In the middle is a six feet pole where the fisher stands, pole against his shoulder; the net spread across the estuary. Fishing time is either when the tide is coming in or going out. If the fisher is fortunate he has waist-high oilskin waders; if not, skin is waterproof.

With a young family to feed and being young, Sandy waded barefoot, 'sark and breeks', into the outgoing water. His favourite site was between two sandbanks on which sat two rotting hulks where in each case the captain had misjudged the tides and run aground. Although the ships sat some twenty yards apart, the channel that ran between was only twenty feet, ideal for placing the haaf-net. In a short time, Sandy had acclimatised to the cold water and was happily pulling fish from his net and placing them in the creel, or basket, on his back. Each time a fish hit the net he could feel a soft thump. He had just been struck by the large thump of a salmon when a light went on in the ship to his left. This was followed by a chopping sound. For a moment Sandy assumed that some poor wretch was attempting to get some free firewood when a light went on in the ship opposite and a harsh, high-pitched voice called out, 'Whit are ye daein?'

'I'm makin a wife fer Sandy McHarg,' called out an equally harsh voice in reply.

It took but a moment for Sandy to realise what was afoot. This was no prank by some young wags, but a sinister scheme by the Sìth-mara, the sea elves – not cute little fairy folk, but malevolent, demonic creatures whose joy was the torment of humans. With all his power he drove for the shore, cast down the creel and net and rushed shoeless for home.

Sandy crashed through the door of his house, slammed it shut and rammed home the two locking bolts. He then slammed home the shutters and bolted them. His wife, who was cooking a stew, stood in shock at all the commotion, 'Sandy whit's gaun on?'

Sandy ignored her, strode over to the sleeping children and, with a little gentleness, hauled them from their bed. He laid them in front of the fire then turned to his wife and said forcefully, 'Get on yer knees, Janet, an pray tae God Aamichty to protect yer immortal saul; confess ilka sin, nae maiter how smaa an beg his forgieness an pertection.' He dropped to his knees and clasped his hands in prayer.

'Sandy, whit is gaun on?'

The young man grabbed his wife's arm and pulled her to her knees, 'Juist dae as I telt ye! Please!' Sandy was afraid that should he convey his fears to his beloved wife the coming enchantments would be fulfilled.

'Sandy, ye're makin me feart.'

'Maybe sae, lass, but whiles there are uncos tae fear. Please, juist dae as I ask.' Their marriage had been, unusually for the time, a meeting of minds, a relationship built on mutual respect, love and trust, so she clasped her hands and set herself in worship.

Over the murmur of their prayers, Sandy heard the sound of an approaching horse. It drew up outside the cottage and then there was the slap of leather boots on the ground. A second later there was a hammering on the door, 'Guidwife, will ye come. The Earl o Dumfries's guidwife is in labour an needs a howdie. Sae ye'll need tae cam noo.'

'Did ye hear that, Sandy? I kentna she wis expectin a bairn. I maun gae an help this instant.'

'Ye'll stey whaur ye are, Janet.'

'But—'

'Stey!' he commanded with finality. 'Since when daes a sixty-year-auld dame beir a wean?'

'In the Guid Buik, Abraham's wife Sarah wis aulder.'

'Aye maybe so, but the Earl o Dumfries is no Abraham. Ye'll stey.'

'Are ye comin, wumman?' called the voice.

'She's no comin,' yelled Sandy. 'Find some ither body.'

'Ye'll pey dearly for this!'

'Aye, maybe so, but she's no comin.'

The sound of creaking leather was heard, then pounding hooves that disappeared into the night.

'They'll get us pit aff oor land.'

'This is ma land, bocht and peyed fer by ma great-grandfaither, so I thinkna, lass.' He laid a fond hand on his wife's shoulder. 'Trust me and keep prayin, Janet. The nicht is nae ower.'

No sooner were the words spoken that a flickering light appeared along the bottom of the door and down the cracks in the shutters. A moment later came the lowing of cows in distress accompanied by the screaming neigh of a horse and the frightened cackling of hens.

'Sandy, the barn's on fire. Whit hae they duin tae us?' Janet rose quickly and ran for the door. Sandy was on his feet instantly and ran and grabbed her, pulling her back to the fire. She struggled to be free, 'Sandy, Sandy, ye've lost yer heid. We'll be paupers on the roads o Gallowa.' She sank to her knees in tears.

He kneeled beside her, drew her head on to his shoulder and gently stroked her hair. 'Sssh,' he soothed, continuing his prayers for them both.

Soon the noise abated and the flickering light extinguished. Being mid-summer, it was not long before another light appeared under the door: that of the coming day. After giving his confused wife a long affectionate hug, Sandy lifted the still-sleeping children back into their beds then opened the door. His wife followed. They both stood and looked at their still-standing barn before they opened the door on to a peaceful stock of animals. As they stepped back into the daylight Janet said, 'Whit wis that aa aboot, Sandy?'

Sandy nodded to something behind her. She turned and immediately put a hand to her mouth in shock, for there, stood against the cottage wall, was a likeness of herself hewn in old timber.

'Whit is it Sandy?'

'It's a sìthbheire, a changeling. Had you gaun oot that door the Sith-mara wuid hae taen ye fer their ain and that thing wuid hae taen yer place.'

'Whit dae we dae wi it?'

'Naethin. We get the meenister tae gie us advice.'

The minister's advice was to build a bonfire, put a pitchfork into the thing and throw it and the pitchfork on to the fire. With the minister and half of New Abbey attending, the bonfire was constructed, lit and the sìthbheire and pitchfork tossed on. As the thing caught fire it suddenly and frighteningly shot up in a column of flame, sending everyone scattering. When the fire had burnt out, Sandy noticed something shining in the ashes. When he retrieved it he found a long-stemmed metal goblet covered in strange ornate designs. Strange as it was, Sandy kept it to remind himself, as if it were needed, what a fortunate man he was to have such a wonderful wife.

The goblet still exists and remains in the McHarg family to this day.

12

The Wife of Lochmaben

The eighteenth century in Scotland was the famous Age of Enlightenment. Giants of the time, like Robert Adam, David Hume, James Watt and Robert Burns put Scotland at the hub of world progress and culture, dragging it out of a dark and violently superstitious past. However, the old world was not so easily converted to the new rationalism and many common folk were resolute in their ways. Collision of beliefs and conflict were inevitable, and in the late eighteenth century a case came before the Circuit court in Dumfries that underlined this conflict.

In the ancient and royal burgh of Lochmaben lived a good and decent Christian woman called Mary Neil. The woman suffered from a painful and debilitating illness that consigned her to bed. This she bore with great stoicism. She was married to a blacksmith by the name of James Neil, who was, in many ways, her complete opposite. He paid his wife little attention and had taken up with a gipsy woman who lived in the same building. While her husband, on the pretext of not wishing to disturb his wife, whiled away his leisure time with his lover, the woman was visited by a neighbouring widow who was also of a religious persuasion. The two women consoled each other with social chat and regular readings from the bible and other religious texts. The kindly neighbour showed great, selfless devotion to her friend. While both were not unwise to the James Neil's degeneracy, indifference and a particular hostility to the widow, he was still included in their prayers and blessings.

As was her daily wont, the widow made her way to Mary Neil's house only to discover her friend was absent. The bed was cold and unmade and the fire unlit, but what alarmed the widow most was that her friend's daytime clothes still lay beside the bed. She ran to the smiddy to alert the husband only to be met with malevolence. 'Gang tae the Deil, ye hypocritical auld jade,' he said, never lifting his eyes from the metal he was furiously beating. She implored the husband to help her look for his wife. 'If ye dinnae ken whaur she is, hoo am I tae ken? If ye wish tae find yer snivelin crony, seek whaur ye saw her last.'

Realising she would get no help from the blacksmith, the widow ran to her neighbours and sought their assistance. The town and its closes and crofts were scoured without success. The search spread further to the surrounding woods and fields until someone saw clothing floating in the loch that gave the town its name. A boat was launched and the rowers found that more than just clothes floated in the water: they contained the body of Mary Neil. Her corpse was dragged to the shore and a visiting doctor from Dumfries, in a hurry to return home, carried out a perfunctory examination. He decreed she had died of drowning; probable cause: suicide.

In no time, rumour spread that the woman, miserable in an unhappy marriage, had thrown herself in the loch in despair. The protestations of the widow were ignored in favour of what seemed obvious. Even in those more enlightened times, suicide was the ultimate sin – murder of one's self – the ultimate act against God. She would now be denied a Christian burial in consecrated ground.

A rough-cut coffin was made with old tools. Once used, they were abandoned. It was then tied with old dispensable rope and dragged by an aged, infirm nag westward to the most remote part of the parish. There on the march, or boundary, a grave was dug and the coffin and ropes consigned to it. The name Mary Neil and her date of death were scratched on a flat stone and this was thrown

in on top of the coffin, then all was covered over. The tainted nag
was marked and set loose to roam free.

After her death, the woman continued to be broadly slandered
and her religious devotion held to ridicule, 'Sae heich an michty
she wis, but in the end she gaed tae the Deil fer comfort. Ye cannae
tell folk frae appearances.' Others had sympathy for the woman,
'There's nae proof she killt hersel, and if she did, wha cuid blame
her wi her illness and that profligate husband o her's and his
"Egyptian".'

The widow herself fell into despair at her friend's apparent action
and abandoned her daily prayers, now doubting heavenly justice
and God's mercy. All her certainties were now dismantled and
life's anchor torn from her; she spent her days in bewilderment. 'I
cannae believe Mary killt hersel: it cannae be richt. But whit ither
answer is there?' Unable to find truth elsewhere, she once again
resorted to prayer, asking God's forgiveness, mercy and an end to
all her doubts as to the true path to Heaven.

Having thus prayed, she fell into a deep grief for her friend, weeping bitter tears of loss. Through her sobbing she heard footsteps and endeavoured to cover her distress. As the figure approached she gasped, as, through her tear-stained eyes, the person so resembled Mary Neil. As the figure drew close she saw that it was indeed her dear companion. 'God preserve us Mary, is that ye?'

'Wha else wuid it be?'

'But ye were droont in the loch.'

'And wha wuid hae droont me?'

'They said ye had droont yoursel.'

'And ye believit them?'

'Weel … aye!'

'Hoo cuid ye dae me sic an injustice? Hae we no been pious in the life we hae shareit, eer myndfuu o the gait tae heiven?'

'Then whaur hae ye been?'

'I hae been on a journey tae a straunge and wunnerfu place. I traivelt bi wey o a cauld, dowie place caaed the Crane Muir.'

'But dear Mary, that wis whaur they buryit the body that was fand droont in the loch. But ye are no deid?'

'Do ye no see me alive and weel and happy and joyfuu?'

'I ken the saul can neer dee but tell me, wis it no yer body that was fand floatin in the loch and that wis buryit in shame and disgrace on the Crane Muir?'

'This wis sae. But, as ye see, I am raisit frae the deid and restorit tae life and aa fer yer sake. Did ye truly believe that I wuid throw awa the precious life I was gien and endanger ma immortal saul bi takin ma ain life?

'I didnae believe it, but wis perswadit itherwyse bi the gossip o ithers. Forgie me.'

'Ah dear freend, ma husband fellt me wi a bottle on the back o ma heid and pit ma body in a seck. He then cairryit it oot of the hoose in the mirk and threw it in the loch. It was a daurk deed that in the fuuness o time he wull repent. Straungely, fer me, it wis an act o mercy as I am noo free o an infirm body. I am weel and happy and safe in the care o oor Saviour.'

On the instance of this revelation, the widow fainted. When she recovered, Mary Neil was gone. Realising she was in a whole state of mind when the vision appeared, she was certain of what she saw, whether it was the ghost of Mary Neil or a spirit in her likeness. This being so, she was resolved to expose the crime.

The following day the widow went to the town magistrate and informed him of what had passed. The magistrate laughed in her face and poured scorn on the matter, saying that she should never again mention it for fear of being deemed insane. She offered to swear to the events on oath, which only served to rile the official all the more. Realising there was nothing to be gained in pushing the matter further, the widow went to her minister, assuming she would get a sympathetic ear. She was shown sympathy but little understanding. The minister also cautioned her to let the matter rest, as she was so obviously under strain and grief at the loss of her dear friend and her imagination had become overactive. She saw that he was so fully convinced in his reasoning that it was pointless to go on. The poor woman now understood that these men of learning belonged to a new and alien world.

This did not prevent her from broadcasting it among the people of Lochmaben who, in a short time, rose as one and demanded that some action be taken. So powerful was their voice that a band of citizens along with two other ministers, two magistrates and two doctors set out for Crane Muir. By order of the magistrates and with due ceremony by the ministers, the body of Mary Neil was exhumed and inspected by both doctors.

The result of the post-mortem was conclusive: Mary Neil had indeed been killed by a blow to the back of the head. The design of the wound seemed to indicate a bottle as being the most likely cause of the injury. So certain was the original doctor of the cause of death that he had omitted to do a full examination. The injury was hidden beneath a thick band of hair bound beneath a snood. This was enough for the crowd, who demanded that Mary be taken to Lochmaben and buried in consecrated ground, as was her due. Her husband was forthwith arrested.

The story of Mary Neil's ghost and her deliverance into the care of the Saviour spread broadly and had churches full in no time. At the circuit court in Dumfries the public gallery was packed to hear the evidence against James Neil. There was complete silence as the widow gave her testimony. Even when cross-examined by the counsel for the defence she never once strayed from her story. It seemed that the result was a foregone conclusion, until Neil's counsel pointed out that the widow was not a first-hand witness, but had the information relayed to her. He said, aided by biting sarcasm, that he would accept his client's guilt were the ghost of Mary Neil to appear in person. The blacksmith was remanded until a later circuit while the prosecution sought a material witness. Such a witness was found, confirming that he had seen a figure carrying a large sack out of James Neil's house on the night in question Further cross-examined by the defence counsel, he admitted that while the figure looked similar in size and proportion to that of James Neil, he had, in fact, not seen his face.

Asked why he had not come forward earlier, the witness said that on the night in question he had been on business of a nature he could not reveal and had to depart for a season until all was well.

In summing up, the counsel for the defence argued with great fluency, not to mention his propensity for sarcasm, that ghosts and unreliable witnesses are not the stuff by which a man is hanged. And besides, a material witness, James Neil's 'Egytian' friend, had sworn on oath that he was with her on that night. The judge, in summing up, said that the proof was defective and that there was no place in law for the supernatural, perhaps conveniently forgetting that people swore on oath before the most supernatural being of all, God himself. He suggested that perhaps the widow, when saying her last farewell to Mary Neil, had discovered the injury or, more likely, had dreamed up the whole matter and, being so convinced of it, had, in her mind, deemed it fact.

In the end, the jury, by a small majority, brought forward a verdict of 'not proven'. The judge dismissed the defendant, but not before expressing his disapproval at the smith's reprehensible conduct.

Now acquitted of the crime, the blacksmith sought to resume his life and business in Lochmaben. Acquitted in the eyes of the law he might have been, but not in the eyes of the good burgh's townsfolk. Once Neil was retired to the arms of his lover, a crowd silently gathered outside then dragged them from the house and forcibly made them ride the stang before giving both a severe ducking in the loch, the scene of his infamy. Both were hounded out of town, only just escaping with their lives. Last heard of in Cumberland, locals were in no doubt that both would come to a bad end.

GHOSTS, SPECTRES, WRAITHS AND POLTERGEISTS

What is a ghost? Is it an earthbound spirit, an unbaptised soul or, as some followers of quantum physics would have it, time past imprinting on the present? Dumfries and Galloway has its fair share of such phenomena. In times past, ghosts were accepted realities.

THE BUCKLAND LADY

To the east of Kirkcudbright, the Buckland burn runs through Buckland Glen down into the Manxman's Lake just south of the town. Long ago, a farmer from Monklands near Dundrennan was on his way home. The farmer was riding a garron and beside him walked a farm lad. As they came downhill to the bridge across the Buckland, the horse shied and almost threw the farmer. At the same moment the lad gasped and pointed. 'See whit's yonner,' he said.

The farmer looked to the road up the hill beyond the bridge that they would take. 'Aye laddie,' said the farmer quietly, 'Whit they say is true enuech. It's the heidless leddy wha wis murdert in the auld Wicked Times. We'll respect her presence and tak the road doon Buckland and up by Gilroanie.' This time the farmer walked so as to comfort his spooked horse.

Curiously, a week later the farmer heard that there were two local ruffians waiting to accost him and relieve him of the money he had just withdrawn from the bank in Kirkcudbright. Had the lady not turned them, it is likely there would have been another tragedy in Buckland Glen.

PHANTOM PIPER OF DUNSKEY

Dunskey Castle is a twelfth-century towerhouse that sits on a cliff half a mile south of Portpatrick and carries with it an air of menace and foreboding. It is now unsafe to enter the building. Perhaps just as well, as it has a reputation of being haunted by more than just one ghost.

The most famous is the 'hairy man' or brownie that is alleged to have been seen in the castle precincts. The second is that of a nursemaid who accidentally dropped her charge on to the rocks one hundred feet below – some say she then threw herself after the child. The third is perhaps the most interesting.

In the fourteenth century, the castle was owned by one Walter de Corry, a violent maritime freebooter. Among his prisoners was a piper who was given the job of de Corry's personal piper and jester. He was, however, fearless and outspoken. In the end, he raised the ire of the laird who decided that he would suffer a lingering death by starvation in the castle dungeons. During his incarceration the piper found a subterranean passage but unfortunately, although he escaped the dungeon, the underground passage led to (literally) a dead end. But this was not the last to be heard of the piper, for thereafter his ghostly piping could at times be heard from underground, marching up and down the hidden passage. Just a tale, many said, until workmen, engaged in another type of piping for Portpatrick's water and drainage scheme, discovered a large hidden chamber from where the music emanated.

THE PHANTOM OF GALDENOCH TOWER

In the seventeenth century, many Scots signed a covenant rejecting the English Episcopalian form of Protestantism for Presbyterianism. This brought about the wars of the Covenant. Although Presbyterianism finally won the day, royalist forces were used to implement Episcopalianism. A force of ill-armed Covenanters from Galloway marched on Edinburgh but was defeated at Rullion Green on the Pentland Hills, a short distance from the city.

The Laird of Galdenoch, one of the defeated Gallovidians, was making his way home to the Rhins and sought shelter at a large house. The owner was a loud-mouthed royalist but hospitable enough to let the laird stay for the night. In the morning his host was in a belligerent mood and accused him of being with the enemy. Seeing he was about to be detained and almost certainly hanged, the young man pulled out his pistol and shot the man dead. He rushed out, saddled his horse and rode hard for home.

There was a celebration at home for his safe arrival where he elaborated recent events. As the night lights were extinguished, another presence was felt, something noisesome and malignant. The laird knew straight away that he had been followed home by the ghost of the man he had killed. Nightly the visitations wreaked fear and dread on the family and finally they fled the building.

The new tenant and his family, unaware of the wraith, were one night playing a fireside game where a lighted stick was passed from hand to hand, the holder reciting:

> 'Aboot wi that! Aboot wi that!
> Keep alive the priest's cat.'

Should the flame go out then a forfeit was expected. What was not expected was the peat in the fire to glow extremely bright, then for one of the blocks to disappear. Moments later a fire started in the thatch of an outbuilding. In the middle of it could clearly be seen the missing peat block. The group very quickly extinguished the flames.

Sometime later, the tenant's mother was at her spinning wheel when she was dragged from her seat by an invisible force and thrown into the mill burn. A disembodied voice could be heard saying, 'I'll dip thee, I'll draw thee.' As it was dinner time, Granny was missed, so the place was searched for her. The disembodied voice was heard again in the house saying, 'I've washed Granny in the burn and laid her on the dyke to dry.' Sure enough, the elderly lady was found on the dyke, stark naked, cold and half dead with fright.

Local ministers were brought in to lay the ghost but none was successful. As the minister and family sang, the ghost outsang them. One minister, a reputed expert at ghost-laying, was brought in but the ghost exhausted his capabilities. Duly insulted, the minister left, swearing, 'I will never cross this threshold again.'

'Come back and gie it ae mair try, meenister.' The minister obligingly returned, only to be taunted by the voice calling, 'Ha! Ha! Ha! I hae gotten the meenister tae tall a lee.'

Eventually the famous Reverend Marshal of Kirkcolm was sent for. He was renowned for having the loudest voice in all the parishes and it was said that when he preached in Leswalt he could be heard at Innermessan on the other side of Loch Ryan, some three miles distant. The zealous minister took on the ghost and by the following morning had outlasted family, neighbours and, most importantly, the ghost, 'Roar awa reverend, I am duin,' came a hoarse voice that was heard no more.

The Ghost of Spedlins Tower

Spedlins Tower, the ancient home of the Jardines, sits the west side of the River Annan five miles north of Lockerbie. The original tower was probably built in the twelfth century but has been rebuilt a number of times, notably in 1605 and again in the 1960s, after being in some disrepair.

In the seventeenth century, it was the home of Sir Alexander Jardine, an affable man who was occasionally quick to anger.

During one of these rages he severely upset his miller, James 'Dunty' Porteous. In a fit of pique, the miller reduced his mill to ashes. In a fury at Porteous's destruction, Sir Alexander threw the miller into the dungeon of Spedlins Tower, a dreaded and dismal place.

At the same time, Sir Alexander had important business to deal with in Edinburgh. He took a route through the Borders, to attend to some other matters on the way. This meant that the journey to Edinburgh took longer than usual. It was not until he reached the West Port of the city some weeks later that he realised he had left his unfortunate miller imprisoned without food. In haste he sent one of his servants riding back to Spedlins. 'Ride, ride and spare neither whip nor rein.'

The attendant rode hard for home but alas was too late. The miller was dead. But what horrified the servant was the fact that in his desperate hunger and thirst, Porteous had gnawed one of his arms to the bone.

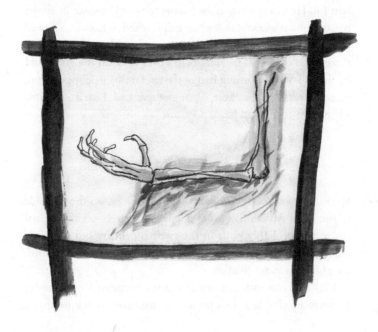

Sir Alexander had no sooner returned to Spedlins than an apparition appeared. A sleeper in the tower would be awakened by a fleshless arm beckoning them to the dungeon. The terrorised staff implored Sir Alexander to have it exorcised. Many ministers arrived and carried out the ceremony but failed to remove the phantom. Finally, by laying a bible by the door, the ghost was consigned to the dungeon. However, the staff were, on occasions, tormented by screams of, 'Let me oot, let me oot, I'm deein o hunger,' followed by a 'fluttering' sound of bones being run across iron bars.

By the nineteenth century, the tower had fallen into disrepair and became the haunt of raptors and ravens that nested among the crown of ivy. At this time a schoolmaster from Dumfries, who was a keen musician and composer, went to visit his friend, the headmaster of Applegarth, passing Spedlins on the way. Entranced by the tower, he spent some time touring its precincts and, consequently, was late. He apologised to his host, explaining the reason for his tardiness. During an evening of music and mirth the Applegarth dominie related the miller's tale. So inspired by the rugged beauty and lore of Spedlins were the gentlemen that they set about composing a piece of music. Once the music was in manuscript form they set off to play the piece in its natural setting.

It was a quiet June evening when they reached the tower, with the sun just hovering above the trees. To get the right atmosphere, they waited until the coming of dusk before descending into the dungeon. Gaining access to where the miller had been incarcerated proved more difficult, loaded down as they were with violin and case, music book and music stand. Using a length of rope they lowered themselves into the vault. The space was claustrophobic, being eleven and a half feet deep, seven and a half feet long and two and a half feet wide. The Applegarth dominie held a candle while the Dumfries man set the music book on the stand. He then awkwardly opened the case, took out the violin and bow and positioned himself with his back to the wall so he could play. With some trepidation he put bow to string and played their first piece, 'The Lament for Flora MacDonald'. The haunting melody swelled about them, filled with deep melancholy and loss. Applegarth could feel the prick of tears and swallowed hard. 'Grand, grand,' he said after the last note died away. He then turned the page, opening it at the new composition, 'The Ghost of Spedlins Tower'. The book seemed to have a mind of its own and turned to 'The Fairy Dance'. The lively notes danced around the tower as did both men in the restricting vault. Both laughed simultaneously at the end. Their laughter was cut short as the book now turned, of its own volition, back to 'The Ghost of Spedlins Tower'. The Dumfries dominie promptly complied.

As the last note on the sixth bar of the music died away, the book, as if turned by an unseen hand, closed; in the same instant the candle was snuffed. As the masters stood unmoving in the impenetrable darkness, a whisper was heard followed by a fluttering sound that gradually died away. All that remained was calm and peace.

THE RERWICK POLTERGEIST

In the seventeenth century a pamphlet was published entitled, 'A True Ralation of an Apparition, Expressions and Actings of a Spirit which infested the house of Andrew Mackie, in Ringcroft of Stocking, in the Parish of Rerwick, in the Stewartry of Kirkcudbright, in Scotland'. It was printed in Edinburgh by George Mosman, and sold at his shop in the Parliament Close in 1696. The pamphlet was written by Reverend Alexander Telfer, the minister of Rerwick Parish.

Ringcroft of Stocking was a smallholding on the topside of Auchencairn in the parish of Rerwick. The tenant in Ringcroft was Andrew Mackie, who farmed the property with his wife and three children. In 1695, it was the scene of either one of the most elaborate hoaxes one could ever perpetrate or, if witnesses are to be believed, a profound case of poltergeist activity. At the time, it was heavily investigated by fourteen eminent members of the community including the Reverend Alexander Telfer, who wrote the account of the phenomenon. It was widely reported and even entered in the *Encyclopaedia Brittanica*.

In February 1695, some of Mackie's cows, which had been tethered in the barn, were found wandering freely on the farm, their tethers having been broken. The next night they were retied with stronger rope but the following morning the ties were broken and the beasts free. No harm had come to the beasts but the event made Mackie wary. Shortly after, when the herd had been purposely left out, a half-ton cow was found suspended by rope at the back of the house, its feet just touching the ground.

What started off as seemingly inexplicable pranks took on a more sinister aspect when a creel of peats was moved to the middle of the floor in the house and set alight. Fortunately, the family was woken by smoke and extinguished the fire. Unaccountable fires springing up all over the farm became commonplace. On Monday, 7 March, stones were thrown at the house, raining on it night and day from all direction until the following Sunday. This continued intermittently for many weeks after. Members of the family and visitors were also subject to stoning; some were badly injured. Another time a hot stone was dropped on the bed between the children and burned through the bedclothes. The stone was removed and dropped on the floor. When the eldest child, a boy, tried to lift it an hour and a half later it burned his hand.

The poltergeist also had a voice, and number of times, during prayers, was heard calling, 'Wheesht, wheesht'; other times, while stones were being thrown, it made a whistling sound followed by, 'Tak that till ye get mair.'

One peculiar case in the affair was when an acquaintance, Andrew Tait, came to spend the night with the family. On the way, his dog caught and killed a 'thulmart' or polecat. He dropped the animal at the door. That evening Tait, and another three young men who were visiting, were beaten about the body with the carcase. One of the terrified visitors had it thrust into his pockets and up under his clothes to such a degree that he fainted.

Mackie was advised to look for signs of witchcraft, for it was known that sometimes aggrieved tenants who had been evicted from a farmstead would carry out a curse on the holding. With this in mind Mackie searched the house then, by accident, his wife noticed that the large, flat doorstep stone was slightly loose. When the stone was lifted they found bones, flesh and blood wrapped in leather parchment. The local laird was appealed to and asked if he would get everyone local to come and touch the bones. Were the guilty person to touch the bones the curse would be lifted. This was done, but to no avail, so ministers were brought in to do an exorcism. This was equally ineffective. More mysterious fires erupted across the farm; even sheep were found with smouldering fleeces. Malevolent threats were made against the family, including one child being pulled out of bed and a large block of wood held over the children with a disembodied voice saying, 'If I had a commission I wuid brain them.'

Literally dozens of incidents were recorded or attested to by witnesses not members of the family. In all, the poltergeist activity ran from February until the end of April 1695 when Andrew Mackie was in the barn and a voice called him, 'Andrew, Andrew.'

Mackie did not reply to it. 'Speak!' commanded the voice. Still the farmer refused to converse. The voice came again, 'Be not trubbelt; ye shall hae nae mair trubbel, except some castin o stanes upon Tuesday to fuufil the promise.' It then added, 'Tak awa yer straw!'

On the Tuesday, several neighbours were in the barn praying when a black cloud-form appeared in a corner. As the visitors backed off, chaff and mud was thrown in their faces. The following day, which was the first of May, a small hut for the sheep caught fire. The sheep were saved but the hut was burned to the ground. And thus ended the visitations of what is known locally as 'The Ghost of Rerwick'.

THE GHOST OF LITTLEMARK

To the south of Sanquhar is the Elliock Estate and on the estate is the farm of Little Mark. The people who ran the farm were Robert and Joseph Graham and their sister Mary. She was a fine-looking lass and was sought after by the young men of the valley, but her heart was devoted to a Sanquhar lad named Andrew Gourlay who was a shepherd on the estate. On the surface the family seemed decent and respectable. In truth, they were a ruthless crew not averse to murder.

One cold evening in late January a pedlar came by the house, his horse loaded with drapery and other fine goods. Light snow was falling so the trader was more than happy to accept the offer of lodgings for the night. That same night Mary Graham had arranged a tryst with young Andrew Gourlay. The lad was early and surprised to see the screens pulled. There was a broken pane in the window through which he could hear a violent struggle so, using his stick, he prised up the curtain. What he saw struck him with horror: the pedlar was being held down and gagged by Joseph and Mary while Robert strangled the poor unfortunate. In alarm he set off for home but his love for Mary kept him from exposing the crime, except to his mother. But now he could no longer bring himself to see her. Later, he met Mary at Sanquhar Fair. She chided him on his failure to arrive for their tryst. He said he had kept the appointment but had come upon the murder and fled. He added that he could never see her again.

The pedlar's horse had been found wandering loose in Elliock Woods but no one had any idea who it belonged to, though someone suggested it might be the result of some nefarious deed. The Grahams felt safe that their crime would never be exposed and went about their daily life as usual. That changed when Mary returned from the fair. The family agreed that though Andrew had said nothing, there was no guarantee that he would remain silent. With that in mind they resolved to murder him too. They discovered that he was to drive a flock of sheep south to near Dumfries, so they set a lookout to watch for his return, which they guessed would be about midnight; the idea was to ambush him at Elliock Bridge.

It was a cold moonlit night as Andrew came down the track. Joseph and Mary lay motionless on either side; Robert hid beside the bridge to cut off any escape. When he was opposite them they rose and attacked, aiming to pull him down and strangle him as they had done the pedlar. However, being a nimble young man, he pulled away, but his escape was cut off by Robert. In desperation, he threw himself into the swollen River Nith. As he went down the water the trio split and trailed him on both sides. Ahead of Andrew was a large rock. He grabbed it and held on, trying to pull himself out of the freezing water. His attackers started to throw stones, aiming at his hands so he would have to let go. Bruised and bloodied, the young man could no longer hold on and slid to his death in the chilling turbulence.

The body of Andrew Gourlay was dragged from the water at Glenairlie, two miles further south. The doctor who attended the post-mortem could make no sense of the battering to Andrew's fingers and head. That was until Andrew's mother accused the Grahams of having a hand in her son's death as a witness to the murder of the pedlar. Sanquhar folk were incensed and set off to apprehend the murderers, but the killers had decided that time was up and had fled.

Soon after, a wailing was heard along the banks of Nith and in Elliock Woods. The soul of Andrew Gourlay would find no rest, as justice had not been done.

Years later, a decrepit vagabond by the name of Beggar Johnnie came to Sanquhar. Someone recognised him as Joseph Graham. When apprehended, he confessed his crime, took a fit and dropped dead. Robert Graham was never heard of again but was rumoured to have died of drink in Dumfries. His sister Mary returned to the parish and took to living in a hut on the moors. Of advanced years, she was avoided as an evil woman until she expired unloved and unlamented. It was then that wailing in the woods and on the river ceased. Justice would be had ... in Hell.

14

BANNOCKS AND PUDDOCKS

The following are two classic tales connected by a common theme: the old way of baking a bannock. This was a kind of large oatcake made from oats or barley, milk or water, butter and salt. The milk or water is heated with butter and salt added, then the oats are poured in and stirred with a spurtle, a long wooden pin, until a thick dough forms. It is then scraped out on to a floured board and kneaded, then rolled until about three quarters of an inch thick. It is then placed on a girdle, a round flat sheet of iron, or a bannockstane, a flat slab of sandstone, set on peat, wood or coal cinders and baked fifteen minutes each side. This was the *bread* of Scotland for hundreds of years: the Gallovidians, who were the vanguard of the Scottish Army, famously marched to battle on it.

The Frog Prince is a tale found as far away as Korea and Sri Lanka and is very common across Europe. There are many other animal bridegroom tales where the heroine or princess marries a pig, a snake, a horse, a monster and most famously a beast – *Beauty and the Beast*. Even the Arthurian tales have the same conceit but this time it is Sir Gawayne who marries the ugly Ragnelle in order to save King Arthur. She is transformed by a kiss. Strangely, none of the traditional Frog Prince tales has the frog transformed by a kiss. It is when the frog is taken to bed by the girl/princess that the transformation is realised. It is likely that Victorian sensibilities, unable to accept the sexual overtones, plumped for a chaste kiss, after Sir Gawayne. In the original version Chambers writes *(here let us abridge a little)*. I have endeavoured to remove this censorship, but have respected modern sensibilities in the version here adapted from Chambers.

I

The story of the Gingerbread Man is common throughout Europe. Germany and Norway have the *Runaway Pancake*, England has a pudding and Ireland has a cake. There is a delightful Russian version where a woman forgets to bless the dough she is kneading and a little devil gets into it. The United States has a *Johnny-cake*, a *Little Cakeen* and, of course, the *Gingerbread Boy* from whence came *The Gingerbread Man*. Scotland has at least four variations of the story and, Scotland being Scotland, it is more fitting that we have a bannock. The story has been with us a long time: one collected by John Francis Campbell for his *West Highland Tales* in July 1859 from Hector Boyd, a fisherman on Barra, is entitled, *Am Madamh Ruadh's am Bonnach Beag, the Red Fox and the Little Bannock*. This version is from Dumfriesshire.

When cockle shells turn tae music bells,	
An chookies *chew tabaccy,*	hens
An birds big *their nests in auld men's beards*	build
Mowdies *will dig up* tatties	moles, potatoes

There was once an old man and an old woman called Sawney and Aggie Yule who lived happily together in a killogie, a kiln for drying grain; the killogie was near to Closeburn close by Thornhill. Although now too old to have a child, they never lost the desire. Having a kiln attached to the house ensured that it was always warm and so they lived and worked in some comfort. Now, one fine day the husband was busy fixing a grain shovel and his wife was knitting when he said, 'Guidwife, wid ye be sae kind as tae rise an bake wan o yer special bannocks?'

'Dae ye ken,' she said, 'I wis juist thinkin the same masel. I cuild dae wi a wee bite tae eat.'

Aggie took down her baking girdle from beside the fire and set it on the glowing wood embers. She then went to the dresser and took out her large wooden baking bowl, took down a pot from beside the fire and carried them into the pantry. She opened the meal ark and with a hornspoon scooped enough barley-meal into the baking bowl for a large bannock along with a small scoop of salt. She then cut a chunk of butter out of the butter barrel and put it in the pot, then added some buttermilk. She put the pot on the fire beside the girdle, brought it to the boil, gradually added the salted barley-meal and stirred it until it was thick dough. Scraping the dough out of the pot, she worked it in her hands until she had formed a large ball. This she placed on the table, rolled it about then began to knead it. As she kneaded the flour she muttered a small prayer:

'As God mouldit Adam frae the cley,
Sae I mould a wee laddie fer us tae enjoy.'

She formed the dough into separate balls, rolled and flattened them, then joined the pieces to form a human shape; then, with the palm of her hand, she patted the dough until it was roughly half an inch thick. She then took the human-shaped bannock and placed it on the hot girdle. After a while it was turned to bake the underside. This done, she took the girdle off the heat and slid the bannock on to the hearthstone to harden. She returned to her knitting.

'My, that's a grand smell,' said Sawney.

'Aye it is, Sawney,' said Aggie. 'Noo wid ye mind risin an turnin it ower tae harden the ither side.'

Sawney was just rising when the wee bannock spoke, 'Dinnae fash, I'll turn masel.'

Sawney fell back in his seat, knocking the shovel over with a clatter; Aggie dropped her knitting and looked at the wee creature, mouth wide open.

The bannock instantly leaped from the hearthstone and ran for the door. On seeing her 'wee bite tae eat' escaping, Aggie was on her feet in an instant, grabbed the wee pot and chased after it. Sawney, with surprising agility, leaped up too, grabbed a frying pan and followed right behind his wife. Even with its short legs the bannock shot down the road at amazing speed, with the old couple in hot pursuit. As it widened the gap, Aggie threw her pot in frustration. This was immediately followed by the pan. Both missed.

Along a dusty track all lined with trees, bushes and flowers full of
*   bumblebees,*
Drystone dykes, walls and hedges; bogs and marshes, reeds and sedges;
Through a wood and into a dell where he saw two women washing
*   clothes in a well:*

'Welcome wee bannock, wee bannock,' quoth thay,
'Tell us wee bannock, whaur are ye frae?'

'I wis chasit an chasit but awa I fore-ran   ran in front
A wee wee wife and a wee wee man;
A wee wee pot and a wee wee pan;
And sae will I ye; an I'se tell ye, I can.'

The wee bannock spun on the spot before rushing off in cloud of dust. Both women rushed after it but the wee thing was too fast for them. In vexation, the first washerwoman threw a wet jumper, the second a wet scarf. Both missed.

On he went all through the day, past folks in the fields cutting the
*   hay,*
Past happy children playing in parks, full of robins, blackbirds and
*   larks;*
He ran and ran all through the morn until he met two threshers
*   athreshing the corn:*

'Welcome wee bannock, wee bannok,' quoth thay,
'Tell us wee bannock, whaur are ye frae?'

'I wis chasit, an chasit; but awa I fore-ran
A wee wee wife and a wee wee man;
A wee wee pot and a wee wee pan;
Twa well-washers, washin their claes   clothes
And sae will I ye; an I'se tell ye, I can.'

He whirled about then sprinted through their barn and out the back door leaving a cloud of chaff. Though the threshers ran at top tilt, the wee bannock was too fast for them. In irritation, one thresher threw a flail and the other a rake. Both missed.

On and on he went on his run, under cloud and under sun
Over meadows, heath and hill, filled with joy, the fun and thrill
Slowly, slowly he slowed to a crawl as he met two dykers building a wall.

'Welcome wee bannock, wee bannock,' quoth thay,
'Tell us wee bannock, whaur are ye frae?'

'I wis chasit, an chasit; but awa I fore-ran
A wee wee wife and a wee wee man;
A wee wee pot and a wee wee pan;
Twa well-washers, washin their claes
Twa barn-threshers, threshin their corn
And sae will I ye; an I'se tell ye, I can.'

The wee bannock wheeled on one leg before bounding over boulders and away leaving the dykers grovelling in gravel. Though the dykers desperately dashed after him, the wee bun was too brisk and beat them. In annoyance, the first dyker threw a mallet, the second a spade. Both missed.

Over the landscape up and down, through hamlets, villages and one
*   small town,*
Up a slope and over a ridge, along a long valley and over a bridge;
All through the warm and balmy weather when he met two women
*   gathering heather:*

'Welcome wee bannock, wee bannock,' quoth thay,
'Tell us wee bannock, whaur are ye frae?'

'I wis chasit, an chasit; but awa I fore-ran
A wee wee wife and a wee wee man;
A wee wee pot and a wee wee pan;
Twa well-washers, washin their claes
Twa barn-threshers, threshin their corn
Twa dyke-diggers delving their dyke   digging foundations
And sae will I ye; an I'se tell ye, I can.'

The bannock leaped in the air and made off over the moor, leaving
the gatherers buried in a blanket of flowers. Though the gatherers
gave chase the wee scone scooted away. In exasperation, the first
gatherer threw her sickle, the second her basket. Both missed.

Onward the bannock ran down the track and never once did he ever
*   look back;*
He barely noticed the land as he passed, how far the horizon in a
*   world so vast;*
Nothing seen, nothing revealed until he stopped by two ploughmen
*   ploughing a field:*

'Welcome wee bannock, wee bannock,' quoth thay,
'Tell us wee bannock, whaur are ye frae?'

'I wis chasit, an chasit; but awa I fore-ran
A wee wee wife and a wee wee man;
A wee wee pot and a wee wee pan;
Twa well-washers, washin their claes

Twa barn-threshers, threshin their corn
Twa dyke-diggers delving their dyke
Twa heather-getherers getherin heather
And sae will I ye; an I'se tell ye, I can.'

The wee fellow hopped over the plough and tore down a furrow leaving the ploughmen mired in mud. The ploughmen set off in pursuit but were slowed down by the soil on their boots. In anger, the first man threw the cutter, the second the ploughshare. Both missed.

Westward he travelled a full moon behind, the sunset before him
    making him blind;
With his arm he shielded the sun from his eyes, when suddenly, to
    his surprise,
While running along straight as an arrow, he fell over two men
    hauling a harrow:

'Welcome wee bannock, wee bannock,' quoth thay,
'Tell us wee bannock, whaur are ye frae?'

'I wis chasit, an chasit; but awa I fore-ran
A wee wee wife and a wee wee man;
A wee wee pot and a wee wee pan;
Twa well-washers, washin their claes
Twa barn-threshers, threshin their corn
Twa dyke-diggers delving their dyke
Twa heather-getherers getherin heather
Twa peerie *ploumen plouin a* rig   small, field
And sae will I ye; an I'se tell ye, I can.'

He sprang over their heads and headed west, leaving the harrowers smothered in soil. The harrowers hurried after him but he held his own. In a rage, the first harrower threw a tine, the second a pullbar. Both missed.

Our little hero kept on his quest, following the sun as it sank in the
    west;
His little heart was full of glee as he ran on blithely, wild and free;
And all around the twittering birds when he came upon two hungry
    herds

'Welcome wee bannock, wee bannock,' quoth thay,
'Tell us wee bannock, whaur are ye frae?'

'I wis chasit, an chasit; but awa I fore-ran
A wee wee wife and a wee wee man;
A wee wee pot and a wee wee pan;
Twa well-washers, washin their claes
Twa barn-threshers, threshin their corn
Twa dyke-diggers delving their dyke
Twa heather-getherers getherin heather
Twa peerie ploumen plouin a rig
Twa haiverin *harrowers, harrowin the* mools   nonsense talk, soil
And sae will I ye; an I'se tell ye, I can.'

Bouyed up with joy, he danced a jig before jumping a ditch and away. The hungry herds hastened after him but he ran headlong down the highway, leaving them huffing and puffing. One ill-humoured herdsman threw his plaidie, the other his crook. Both missed.

Ever on the wee chiel flew, on past a weasel chasing a shrew,
A kestrel, a kite a buzzard and owl, each of them busy out on the
    prowl,
Past a great eagle perched on high rocks when suddenly the bannock
    ran into a fox:

'Welcome wee bannock, wee bannock,' quoth he,
'Tell us wee bannock, whaur are ye frae?'

'I wis chasit, an chasit; but awa I fore-ran
A wee wee wife and a wee wee man;
A wee wee pot and a wee wee pan;
Twa well-washers, washin their claes
Twa barn-threshers, threshin their corn
Twa dyke-diggers delving their dyke
Twa heather-getherers getherin heather
Twa peeerie ploumen plouin a rig
Twa hungry herds herdin a hirsel   flock of sheep
And sae will I ye; an I'se tell ye, I can.'

Now a fox is a fox, we know that is true, and foxes do what all
    foxes do,
Some say they're sly, some say they're smart, for practice has made
    them skilled in their art,
It's all without malice, umbrage or spite, so the fox ate the bannock
    with one quick bite.

And now for the moral, if a moral it be
If you meet an old fox, don't go bragging, just flee.

II

A young man's father died and left him his small estate. The new laird, whose name was Alexander – Sandy to his friends – decided he would be the man that his father was. His father had been autocratic, arrogant and something of a bully to those around him; especially to women, whom he thought of as second-class citizens. His mother, a good and kind woman, had died of consumption when Alexander was just a boy. Alexander had something of her about him but felt that his father's way must be the right way – his father had told him as much.

Many of the workers on the estate were glad to see the back of the old laird and hoped for better from Alexander. They were to be disappointed. Alexander wanted to prove he was all the man his father was. However, the old laird was naturally mean; Alexander had to work at it and consequently was even more bumptious. He devised new plans for the estate and when his factor protested that it was unviable, he sacked the man. Later he threw an old couple out of their cottage as he deemed them too old to be of use any more. He closed the estate school – his father's one act of decency – for being a drain on his finances. As the estate faltered he blamed everyone but himself, much in the manner his father had done before him. Like the old laird, he treated everyone with disdain and most especially women. When with his friends he would try to outdo them in all things, especially chasing young women, and gained a reputation as a Romeo. In his quiet hours he would chastise himself for his meanness; he would then hear his father's voice rebuking him as being weak. He spent many a night in torment.

It was a cold, sleety day when Meg o the Moor came down from the hills above Moniaive to spend the cold season by the coast. Her winter home was in a half-thatched former cot house on the edge of the estate. She lived off shellfish and the kindness of local people. In return, she cured many an illness with her knowledge of herbs and roots. She had been tolerated by the old laird for she had once eased his gout with apple vinegar and cherries. Alexander had no gout and when he found out she was living on his land rent-free he went to evict her. He rode up to the semi-derelict cottage and shouted on her, 'Are ye in there Meg? Come oot!'

The old woman came to the ramshackle door and leaned on her stick. 'It's yersel, young Sandy. Whit can I dae fer ye. Are ye ill, young sir?'

'Indeed, I am no ill and I dinnae need yer cantrips. Whit I need is for you tae vacate this hoose eenou. That is unless ye are prepared to pey a bawbee fer each week ye stey here.'

Meg looked at the young man calmly and said, 'Ye ken yer faither said I cuid stey here as lang as I liked; an fer nae kane either.'

'Aye well, he's deid. Noo be aff wi ye. That is unless ye hae the kane.'

'Ye are an arrogant young man an deservin o a lesson in guid manners.'

In a fury Alexander raised his whip. He did not intend to hit Meg but rather to frighten her. With an unexpected speed she raised her stick and his arm froze in mid-air. His eyes widened in horror, so sure was he that he was about to be spellbound and subjected to the horrors of Hell.

'Ye hae something o yer faither aboot ye, young Sandy; but I sense that deep in yer hert is the guidness o yer mither. I think ye need a wee bittie time tae fellthocht that.' She stepped up to the catatonic Alexander and touched his waist with her stick. He instantly turned into a frog. Meg reached up to the saddle and lifted him down and dropped him into the pocket of her pinafore. She then went inside and gathered up her bonnet and cloak and set out on a journey.

As she walked she talked. 'We womenfolk hae lang hud tae pit up wi menfolk thinkin they are somethin special; aye, an there's mibbe a few womenfolk that think the same. But ye see, Sandy, yer mither cairryit ye inside her belly and grew ye intae a fine strong lad; she sufferit unimaiginable pain tae bring ye intae the warld; she nursit ye frae her ain breist an she wipit yer erse foreby. Noo is that no worthy o respect? I ken weel that the fate o a man is hard tae, oot there tryin tae provide fer their faimily. But the wifie is no exactly relaxin at hame wi her seiven weans and a supper tae pit on the table; aye, an whiles oot workin in the fields aside their men as weel.'

Meg was now in her stride, both physically and mentally. Her talk was as brisk as her walk. 'An talkin aboot these men and women that wark fer ye i the faulds an the rigs. They are no slaves. They are human beings that have the richt tae be treatit wae respect. Ye can only mistreat folk fer a while an then they fecht back. If ye dinnae gie them that respect, in the end they will disrespect ye and fin weys tae get back at ye. Wis it no the Lord Jesus Christ that said there were eleiven commandments and the eleiventh wis, "I command ye tae luv ane anither"?'

Meg's path led through a wood of silver birches that danced above her head and threw spangles of light across her old shoulders. 'We are nearly there laddie: the Warl's End.' She felt the frog get agitated. 'Dinnae loss yer heid, wee thing; at least no yet.' She patted her pocket. 'Och! Here we be.' She lifted the frog out of her pocket and held him in the palm of her left hand. 'Ye see, here is the Well at the Warld's End. Fer this is the end o yer auld warld, Alexander. Frae here yer fate hinges on ye.' Meg sat down on the stone at the well's edge, and looked into the spring boiling up three feet below, 'Doon there is yer new hame and yer hame it will be intil somebody agrees tae mairry ye. But, mair importantly, tae honour that agreement and tae show ye she cuid lue ye. Aye, an that's no aa. Ye see, the only wey ye can show yer love tae her is tae lose yer heid ower her; sae tae speak. Whit I mean is that unless she chaps aff yer heid, the spell remains.'

The frog's head moved vigorously from side to side as if saying, 'No!'

Meg ignored him and continued. 'Noo ye will ask yersel, "Hoo can I get someone tae agree tae mairry me? An even if I cuid, wuid they chap ma heid aff? An if they chap ma heid aff wuid I be free or deid?" Weel, Sandy. Dinnae think on juist whit I hae said this meenit, think on aa I hae said. Ye'll hae plenty o time.' Gently she dropped the frog into the well. 'I'll be seein ye!' she said before turning and striding purposefully away.

A mother was baking bannocks but had no milk, so instead she decided that, although not as tasty, water would do instead. She called for her daughter to fetch a bucket and go down to the Well at the World's End to get some – it was said that there the water was the sweetest anywhere. After the usual protest the lass found the wooden pail and wandered through the woods on her way to the well in the meadow beyond. It had been a long hot summer – the sun had come out in April and was still shining in August. The well was dry. Now Elsbeth, as her mother had called her, was a lass who could make the greatest drama out of the most minor of crises, so she fell to the ground and wailed. After noting that no one was there to pay her attention she stopped, dried her eyes and was just about to get up when a frog leaped out of the well. Such a fright did she get that she quite fell over. Lifting herself on to her left elbow, she looked at the creature, which looked back at her with what looked like a smile. 'Why are ye greetin?' asked the frog. Such a fright did Elsbeth get that she quite fell over again. The frog waited patiently until she had once more raised herself up on to her elbow. The frog cocked its head to the side, as if to say, 'Well, what's your answer?'

'I wis greetin because ma mither sent me tae the well fer watter, and there's nae watter.'

The frog gave her a long look then said, 'If ye want watter frae the well, ye'll hae tae mairry me.'

She laughed. 'Whit?'

'I said, the only wey I can gie ye watter frae the well is fer ye tae agree tae be ma wife.'

Elsbeth shrugged her shoulders, 'If that's whit it taks tae get watter then, aye, why no? I'll be yer wife.' She suppressed the desire to laugh, but merely grinned.

The frog leaped back into the well and immediately it began to fill with water. When it was deep enough, Elsbeth kneeled down, filled the bucket, stood up and walked away home without barely a thought for the frog, except that she did not take the vow seriously. She would have agreed to anything to get the water and besides, she thought, 'Wha cuild mairry a puddock?'

At home, her mother took the water and put it in a pot to heat. She made up dough with oatmeal, salt, water and butter and cooked it on her bannockstane. While still hot, they spread on butter and cheese and gorged themselves, even licking their fingers. Night was on them so they snuffed the candle and went to bed. Being a very small house, mother and daughter shared the one bedroom, which was also the sitting room and the dining room and the kitchen.

'Guid nicht, mither,' said Elsbeth.

'Guid nicht, lass,' said her mother.

Their heads had only touched the pillow when they heard a scratching at the door. This was followed shortly by the tiniest of knocks that in the daytime they would never have heard. Both listened and waited. Then came a wee gentle voice singing:

'O open the door, ma hinnie, *ma* hert,   honey, heart
O open the door ma ain true luv;
Remember the promise that ye an I made,
Doon i the meidae *whaur we twa met.'*   meadow

'Whit's that noise at the door?' asked the mother.

'Houts mither, it is naethin but a dirty auld puddock.'

'Open the door fer the puir wee thing,' said the mother.

'But it's a—'

'It's wan o God's craiturs,' said the mother, 'an I'll no hae ony dochter o mine mistreatin sic a thing.'

The daughter relented and opened the door. She watched as the frog hopped over to the fireplace and settled in the inglenook. It seemed to smile at her then began to sing again:

'O gie me ma supper, ma hinnie, ma hert,
O gie me my supper ma ain true luv;
Remember the promise that ye an I made,
Doon i the meidea where we twa met.'

'The wee thing maun be stervin,' said the mother. 'Gie it a wee bit supper, hen.'

'I'll dae nae such thing. Ye are encouragin it, mither.'

'He micht be a puddock, but he is a guest in ma hoose an as such is deservin o oor mense. Sae get him a wee bowl o brose.'

The daughter did as she was commanded, but not without gripes and grumbles.

'O tak me tae thy bed, ma hinnie, ma hert
O tak me tae thy bed, ma ain true luv;
Remember the promise that ye an I made
Doon i the meidae whaur we twa met.'

'I will dae nae sic thing,' said Elsbeth, deeply affronted.

'Did ye mak a promise tae the wee thing?'

Elsbeth didn't answer for a moment but could not lie to her mother. 'Aye,' she admitted.

'Then tak the wee thing tae yer bed. Whit herm wid it dae?'

The girl bent down and picked up the frog, wincing at the waxy feeling of its skin. It seemed to smile at her again as she climbed into bed.

'O pit me tae yer breist, ma hinnie, ma hert,
O pit me tae yer breist, ma ain true luv;
Remember the promise that ye an I made,
Doon i the meidae whaur we twa met.'

Elsbeth could not speak, so shocked was she as to what the frog was suggesting that she could only give a strangulated moan.

'Oh the wee thing must be cauld,' said her mother. 'It helpit ye in yer time o need, sae gie it a wee cuddle an keep it warm.'

Elsbeth lay stunned as the frog snuggled into her. But after a while both lay in peace, gently falling asleep. In her dreamy state she stroked the frog's amphibian skin, finding it strangely comforting.

As they all stirred in the morning, the puddock sang again:

'Noo fetch an aix *ma hinnie, ma hert,* axe
Noo fetch an aix ma ain true luv;
Remember the promise that ye an I made,
Doon i the meidae whaur we twa met.'

Feeling more disposed to the frog, Elsbeth went out to the woodyard at the back of the house and fetched an axe.

'Noo chap aff ma heid ma hinnie, ma hert
Noo chap aff ma heid ma ain true luv;
Remember the promise that ye and I made,
Doon i the meidae whaur we twa met.'

Elsbeth stood looking down at the frog that was now on the floor, legs splayed and his head pulled forward in submission.

'I cannae dae that,' she said, though something in her seemed to say it was right to do.

Her mother, who was wise in the lore of life, said, 'Sometimes ye hae tae trust tae Providence. Whit else wid mak a puddock speak? Besides, it is the wee beastie's ain request.'

Elsbeth raised the axe and brought it down hard on the neck. She closed her eyes at the last instant not wishing to see her bloody handiwork. She turned away, dropped the axe and raised her left hand to her mouth as the sobs began. She felt a comforting hand on her shoulder, then a voice said,

'Turn aroon ma hinnie, ma hert,
Turn aroon ma ain true love
Remember the promise that ye an I made
Doon i the meidae whaur we twa met.'

Slightly bewildered, Elsbeth turned about to see a fine and handsome young man. Her bewilderment changed to wonder and joy as she recognised the smile.

The young man confided in them all that had gone before. How he had asked so many young maidens who had all understandably run off in fright. How he had pondered long and found the goodness within himself that lies at the heart of everyone. What had truly sealed it for him was the wisdom, the unquestioning kindness and the hospitality of Elsbeth's mother.

In time, Elsbeth and Alexander were married. The estate, which was nearly lost in his absence, was revived with the old factor reinstated. The old couple returned to their cottage to live out their days and Meg o the Moor's winter abode was renovated and reroofed. Alexander thereafter lived a good life until the end of his days. In all that time, he showed great love and, in return, was loved.

15

SANCT NINIAN AND THE TWA HERDS

Christianity came early to Galloway, probably brought by the Romans before they departed Britain in AD 410. The place most associated with the faith in Galloway is the famous town of Whithorn, from the Anglo-Saxon, Whit Hearne – the White House, or to give it its Latin name, Candida Casa. The person most associated with Candida Casa is St Ninian, an almost mythological figure who lived and preached there in the fourth, fifth or possibly sixth century AD. There is much debate about who he really was, though it is generally agreed that his British name was Uinniau or Finnian. A scribal error had him dubbed Nynia hence Ninian – his name is often found in other guises: Ringan, Ronan, Winning, Trynnian. Ninian was said to have converted the Southern Picts to Christianity (there is much debate as to whether the Picts were in Galloway or that Ninian travelled north of the Forth). However, if you travel the length and breadth of Southern Scotland you will find many wells dedicated to the saint. In his biography, *Vita Sancti Niniani* by Ailred of Rievaulx (which drew from an earlier anonymous eighth-century manuscript *Miracula Nynie Episcopi, The Miracles of Bishop Ninian*), he is attributed with ten miracles, six in his lifetime and four posthumously. Others have appeared in the folklore of Galloway.

In the time of Ninian, southern Scotland was divided into many kingdoms. The mightiest of these was Ystrat Clutha, Strathclyde, with its impregnable fortress at Alt Clut, Rock of the Clyde – what the Gaels called, Dun Brythen, Fort of the Britons – Dumbarton. The king was called Tutagual, who was the father of the much better known Rhydderch Hael, Roderick the Generous. Rhydderch would himself befriend and be a benefactor to the great St Kentigern, otherwise known as Mungo, the beloved.

Ninian had travelled to Alt Clut to convert the pagan Britons. He was generally well received but experienced hostility from Tutagual, the ruler of Ystrat Clutha. The king was a rich, powerful man and full of pride. He did not like the idea of anyone else claiming the affections of his people. Not wishing to openly offend Ninian, whom he considered some kind of wizard, he privately mocked him and generally undermined his mission. Then one day Tutagual was stricken by withering headaches; his vision blurred and then deteriorated into blindness. In the ways of the time, a king who is blind could not lead his army so could not be a king. Druids were called from all over his kingdom, but none could find a cause or a cure. When all had failed, Ninian took pity and offered his healing. At first the king was scornful, but after one more agonising night he relented. Ninian entered the royal chamber and greeted the king warmly. Tutagual merely grunted and rolled over in pain, his hands to his head. Ninian calmly walked over, stood above the tormented regent and prayed to God for the power of healing. As he felt the Holy Spirit flow through him, he placed a hand on either side of the king's head and let God's power flow into the man's brain. The moaning stopped, so Ninian made the sign of the cross over each eye and the king opened them. He sat up grinning, to the delight of all in the room. 'Would you kindly leave us,' he said to his attendants. When they had cleared the room, the king said, 'There are some things my people must never see me do.' He dropped to his knees, and holding Ninian's cloak, begged forgiveness.

Ninian placed his hands on the king's head. 'May the blessing of God, the blessing of his son Jesus Christ and the blessing of the Holy Spirit be with you forever and always. Amen.'

Tutagual rose to his feet and looked at Ninian. 'I have been with the old ways since I was a child, but as a king I should have had the vision to look further than my own beliefs and prejudices.'

'You have, Your Majesty. And when you kneeled, it was not to me; it was to Almighty God and that we must all do. Even in the presence of those we rule over, for he rules over all.'

And so when Tutagual's body was healed, so was his spirit.

A young woman who, as Ailred says, was 'fair of face, graceful of aspect and sinful of flesh' was pursued by an 'unchaste' young man. He was seized by blind love for the girl and in the end overcame any resistance. The result was that she became pregnant. In the beginning she did her best to hide her circumstance for she knew that in those harsh times she would at best be banished and at worst be put to death. Caught in a cleft stick, she chose a desperate plan. When confronted with her alleged sin, she claimed that she had been violently forced into submission by someone of a great name. When urged by the elders to confess who the guilty man was, she claimed it was the presbyter whom Ninian had delegated to care for the parish. The claim was met with horror and disbelief by the elders, the people of the parish and not least by the poor priest himself. Good people were scandalised, the bad gossiped furiously, mocking the Holy Church for its hypocrisy. Everyone was outraged. Everyone, that is, except Ninian who, by revelation, knew the brother monk to be innocent. It was demanded that he take action. He said he would, but as the charge against the presbyter was liable to be a capital offence he needed time. In the meantime the priest would be confined to holy quarters.

Though frustrated with the damage being done to the church, Ninian bore it with stoicism; he was waiting for the inevitable birth of the child. Because of high infant mortality, a newborn was christened within three days of birth and he would personally officiate at the service. The priest would also be required to attend.

On the day, the priests and the baptised entered the church to await the arrival of the baby, her mother and her family; with them came the true father of the child. The girl boldly marched into the church and thrust the baby into the arms of the horrified brother. 'It's your child. You can have it baptised.' The chapel was in uproar.

Ninian raised his arms and with quiet authority calmed the congregation. 'Let us maintain dignity in the presence of God and the innocent child before us.' He then took the baby in his arms and poured holy water over the child's head. 'In the name of the father and of the son and of the holy ghost I command you to speak and say if this man here is your father.' Ninian pointed at the presbyter who looked on in a daze.

The child's head turned in the direction indicated. 'No!' he said clearly. He then pointed to the young man who had begat him and said, 'That is my father.'

A tangible force moved through everyone in attendance and all fell to their knees in awe at the holy presence.

The young man and woman were banished to Ireland and the child taken into the care of the church. In time, the innocent presbyter did indeed become as a father to the child.

❧

Ninian arrived in the refectory at Candida Casa to find that there were no vegetables set out for dinner. He called the monk responsible for the gardens. 'Why are there no leeks set out for the brothers today?' he enquired.

'I am sorry, Your Grace, but I have only just dug and planted out the seeds in the garden.'

'I see,' said Ninian. 'No matter, just go and gather what is there and bring it here.'

'But—'

Ninian raised his hand and silenced the young man, smiled and pointed to the door. The gardener did as he was bid and went to the garden. He arrived to find that the seeds he had planted

❧

had fully grown, some with seedheads that could be replanted. Immediately he fell to his knees and thanked God for working miracles through his devoted servant, Ninian. He then filled a trug and took it to the bishop.

The brothers were amazed and all fell to their knees and prayed, giving thanks to God and to Ninian. The leeks were cooked and served, all observing that they were the best they had ever tasted. It is said that when they departed for evening prayers their souls had been better fed that their bellies.

As well as having an extensive garden, the monastery also employed shepherds, cowherds and henwives to look after their extensive flock of domestic animals. While Ninian preferred to trust the brothers and their staff to do their jobs, he also liked to visit them to show that he cared for all his people. Much of the grazing was spread over a wide area, so a gathering was held every three months at the centre of the Machars near Bryngylfinir, now known as Whaup Hill, the Hill of the Curlew. The distance required that Ninian stay at one of the cowherd's dwellings overnight.

The animals were driven from all the church farmsteads, arriving on the day of the full moon. It took all the way through to sunset for the animals to arrive and for the bishop to inspect them.

When it was over, everyone celebrated before finding a dwelling to spend the night. Instead of placing guards, Ninian took his staff and scored a circle around the gathered beasts. 'Tonight they will have God's protection.'

In the middle of the night, when all were asleep, a band of thieves, aware of the gathering, came from the north intent on driving away as many cattle as possible. To their amusement and delight they found the beasts settled for the night and no one to guard them. Under the light of the full moon, the gang silently entered the circle. Spears at the ready, they moved towards a large white bull, meaning to drive him first. They were within twenty yards of the beast when it turned and charged the group before they had a chance to use their weapons. The group's leader missed his footing and fell. The bull was upon him, crashing down with such force that his hoof marked the rocky ground as if it were wax. The massive horns caught the man full in the stomach. In a panic, the remainder of the thieves made to run but found that they could not pass back over the circle. They spent the rest of the night in a panic, keeping out of the way of the irate beast.

Early the following morning, Ninian went out among the cattle for morning prayers. He discovered the thieves still in a frenzy. When they saw him they threw themselves at his feet begging forgiveness. When he saw the dead leader, his intestines scattered about him, he was filled with remorse that his action had led to the man's death. He prayed earnestly to God to raise the man back to life as the Good Shepherd Jesus had raised Lazarus. It seemed that the heart of God had hardened against the man who had violated his holy circle. Ninian entreated the Almighty but to no avail until his most faithful servant shed tears. God took pity, restored the man to life and made him whole again. The man begged forgiveness and remained a faithful and devoted servant of Ninian and Almighty God until the end of his days.

Now, near the monastery was a school to which the sons of many chieftains from around Galloway and beyond came to learn how to read and write, how to manage clerical matters and how to dispense justice. One young man was of a wild and carefree nature and did not settle well into organised life. Often he would sneak into the village to drink at the local hostelry as well as have assignations with the local girls. Eventually he was to be hauled up before Ninian to account for his behaviour. As he waited outside the bishop's office, he noticed that Ninian's walking staff was leaning against the doorpost and an idea formed in his head. He grabbed the staff and ran off to the bay at the Isle of Whithorn, four miles away. Home was across the Iena Estuary to the Deva Estuary by way of the Ros, some three leagues away. If he could just find a small boat he could row the distance in four or five hours. The wind was from the south-west, so that would help.

At the Isle he could only see a currach, a wicker boat, but no paddle. He had Ninian's staff so decided to go with it anyway. He pushed it from the shore and leaped aboard. His naivety showed, for he had not noticed that the boat was not covered in its usual animal skin. As the water seeped in he intuitively pressed the staff on to the frame; the water withdrew. Cautiously he lifted it like a sail and the boat began to speed over the water. Deciding that to chance his luck in open water was, perhaps, foolhardy, he put the staff over the side where it became as a rudder and guided him back to the shore where a group of people stood in awe at what had just occurred.

Meekly, he stepped ashore, pulled the craft on to the beach and stuck the staff into the ground in relief at his deliverance. 'May this staff, filled with the Holy Spirit, come forth and live once again.' No sooner said than bark appeared along its length and branches erupted from its body. From the branches, leaves and flowers sprouted and a spring of water poured out from under the roots, which later proved to be health giving. Filled with righteousness, the lad walked back to Candida Casa. He knocked on the bishop's door and when called to enter he went in to confess. Ninian greeted him warmly. 'The Prodigal Son returns. I trust you enjoyed your brief life as a sailor.'

'No, Your Grace.'

'Then your time was wasted and we are not here to waste the little time that the Lord God has granted us. Can I presume that you have learned a lesson?'

'Yes, Your Grace.'

'Then the time was not wasted, for you were sent here to learn. God has many ways to teach us the mystery of his ways.'

The boy smiled at Ninian's wisdom, thankful that the experience had taught him something of the power of God and his saints. He was also glad that he had escaped the punishment he had come prepared for.

Ninian smiled back. 'I know you came expecting to be punished and who am I to disappoint? For the next week you can look after the pigs, clean the sties, and when that is done you can find suitable hides, tan them and cover the curragh down at the Isle. But don't think of it as punishment; think of it as a lesson.' He smiled again, 'And close the door behind you.'

'Yes, Your Grace,' he said humbly, learning another lesson about leadership.

In time, the boy's ancestors would become the lords of Galloway, ruling it from their fortress in the middle of Loch Fergus high above the ancient river known as Deva or the Dee.

On the slopes above where the rivers Dee and Tarff converge near Kirkcudbright is Saint Ringan's Well. Near the well is the Boreland, the land dedicated to providing food for the table, or board, at Cumston Castle. The shepherd, who lived at Mid-Boreland, maintained a large flock of one hundred sheep, including the grown lambs of the past summer. To help him with the task was a young herd of fourteen years and two dogs. The two herds together had done a first-class job of maintaining a healthy stock and kept them free from the predations of the wolves that still roamed the hills. Now that winter and the Yuletide was upon them, the weather had deteriorated, so the sheep had been brought down to the lower slopes, and because of the growing hunger of the wolves, the sheep were folded at night in the dry-stone bucht that both herds kept in good order. Built into the bucht was a small single-room dwelling that was the home of the young herd. Containing no more than a bed and a fire in the middle of the floor, the young man was proud that it was his alone and kept it always tidy and clean. He also ensured that his bed was made and his cauldron, wooden bowl and horn spoon were washed and put on the stone shelf that formed part of the wall. On the shelf he also kept his oats and the last of his barley, along with dried berries, salt and a small bone with a little smoke-dried meat on it that the older herd's wife had given him for his Christmas Eve supper.

It was on Christmas Eve when the older herd said to the younger, 'Weel lad, ye are as guid a prentice as I hae had the pleesure tae work wae. Ye are diligent an honest, an when ma lads grow tae manhood, I hope I can be as prood o them as I am o ye.' He smiled at the young herd, who looked at the floor in embarrassment. 'The Magi brocht unco gifts tae set afore the baby Jesus, and wert I sic a rich man I wid gie ye a giftie equal tae yer wirth. God Aamichty has no seen fit tae reward me wi muckle pelf, but there is a giftie I wid like tae bestow on ye, and that is the care o oor flock on this comin haly day. Whit dae ye say?'

Barely concealing his delight, the lad blurted out, 'Sir, it wid be the greatest honour. Bless ye and yer faimily at this guid Yuletide.'

'Tae be honest laddie, it is a giftie fer baith o us. Noo I can be wi ma family at this byordinar time. Sae that can be yer giftie tae me.' The older man laughed and clapped the younger on the shoulder, 'Noo stop yer loupin aboot an awa an bucht the puir beasties afore they freeze tae daith. The snaw is comin on.'

With a brief nod of his head, the young man pulled the hood of his threadworn cloak over his head, turned and ran off up the hill, at the same time whistling to the dogs. Within half an hour the young herd and his dogs had gathered the sheep and were driving them towards the buchts. With the dogs holding the flock in place, the herd removed the gate, stepped back and whistled; the dogs now drove the sheep in as the herd counted, 'Ninety-eight, ninety-nine ...' He looked about him for the missing ewe, but none was to be seen. 'I hae miscoontit!' he said, as a curse. He had no choice but to drive them from the bucht and recount. This he did. 'Ninety-eight, ninety-nine,' he said, this time with an edge of desperation in his voice. The light was failing, the snow was thickening and he was in a panic: the first time he had responsibility for the flock and he had lost a sheep. He would lose more than the sheep. He would lose his job and the meagre income that his mother, with four other children, depended on.

Setting one of the dogs at the gate, he ran up the hill again, sending the other dog hither and thither in search of the errant sheep, but without result. The light was all but gone as he made his way back to the bucht. Dejected, he set down two cogs of oatmeal and milk for the dogs in their willow shelter at the bucht entrance and went into his house, throwing his now damp cloak on the bed. 'Gaun back up the brae wid be madness in this snaw, but I need tae dae somethin,' he said to himself as he lit a cruisie from the embers of the fire he had set at midday. He dragged back from the fire the small cauldron of barley brose he had set to slow cook at the same time. He spooned the brose into his bowl then sat on his bed to eat. 'May as weel gie this tae the dugs.' An idea formed in his mind: 'Gie it tae Sanct Ringan and ask him for help.' It was his only hope and, perhaps, at this special time he might get the help he needed.

He pulled his cloak about him, picked up the brose-filled bowl and spoon and stepped out into the snow-laden night. Head bowed and the bowl held beneath the cloak, he took the well-trodden track to the well. There was just enough light enhanced by white snow to see the water as it tumbled from the hillside over a small wall made to form a pool of water. He laid the bowl at the edge of the wall, pulled back the hood and bowed his head. 'Dear Sanct Ringan, faithfu servand o the sweet baby Jesus, please help me in ma hour o need. I hae lost a yowe frae ma flock. Please tell this puir uiseless sinner whaur he micht find it. Amen.' He stood there in the still night as snow fell silently on his head and shoulders waiting for a sign. Nothing could be heard but the steady slop of the water. 'Please!' he whined in desperation. There was no reply. He looked at the bowl of brose, water now forming on it from melted snow. 'Hae it!' he said in resignation, 'I hae nae need o it noo.'

With his hair streaming melted snow, he gave a long sigh and turned for home. He had taken four slow steps when a voice from behind said, 'Man, this is a grand bowl o brose. Juist the stuff tae keep a puir pilgrim on the road.' The herd spun about and saw an elderly, lank-haired, heavily bearded man dressed in the ragged habit of a religious traveller.

'Whit?' said the surprised young man.

'I'm sayin this is a fine bowl o brose I hae here. Wuid ye care to share?'

'Eh, no! Hae it yersel.'

The man lowered the spoon from his mouth. 'Ye seem fasht laddie. Whit ails ye?'

Ashamed to reveal his seeming carelessness, the young herd shook his head. 'Nuthin,' he said.

'Then tell me whit the nuthin is, lad. I'm an auld man, but I still hae a sound ear tae listen tae whit fashes ye,' said the pilgrim, kindly.

'Eh … it's juist … I was gied a job to luik efter my maister's flock and … and I've lost yin o his yowes.'

The man nodded, 'An like the guid shepherd ye've come tae find it.'

'Aye; exceptin I havnae.'

'No?' said the traveller. 'It widnae be that puir beast that is cleekit tae thae brammle bushes doon there?' He pointed to a small hollow to his left. The herd couldn't make it out with snow now covering everything. 'Ye awa doon an get it, an I'll juist feenish ma wee repast.'

The herd walked to the hollow and slid down the side. Closer, he could see the struggling sheep. He grabbed a horn and slowly dragged the ewe free. As he tried to pull it up the slope, the crook of a stick caught the other horn and both herd and sheep were hauled up. The traveller handed the bowl and spoon to the herd, bent over and grabbed both front and back legs of the sheep; with ease he lifted the animal on to his shoulders. 'If ye can juist bring ma stick, we'll get this lost saul back tae her freends.'

The herd followed in awe as the man strode down to the bucht, opened the gate with one hand and deposited the sheep inside. He closed the gate and, with a smile, took his stick from the herd.

'Hou can I thank ye?' said the herd.

'Ye hae, laddie, ye hae.'

The herd opened the door of his house and stepped inside, dropping the bowl by the fire which had burst into flame, presumably from the opening of the door, 'Ye'll come in, sir. I think there's a wee bit brose left in the pot and ye are welcome to stey the nicht.'

'Thank ye, but no, no, I need to be on ma wey; I'm late as it is.'

'Whaur are ye gaun? Whithorn?'

'Naw, lad, I've juist come frae there.'

'Whaur dae ye need to be sae urgently on Christmas Eve?'

'Bethlehem, laddie, Bethlehem.' The stranger smiled and stepped away.

The young herd stepped quickly to the door, 'But—'

There was no one there, just the gently falling snow and the darkness. He peered deeper into the night. The stranger was gone.

A little baffled, the herd walked to the gate of the bucht, patted the dogs, settled them down then returned to his room, closing the door behind him. The fire burned bright and warm and welcoming. But better still was the pot, full of meat and vegetable-laced brose that sat steaming beside it.

GLOSSARY

Notes on pronunciation: an 'o' is always pronounced as an 'o' never as 'aw'; the 'aw' sound does appear, but only with an 'a' as in, 'fer aa that an aa that'. Good, here spelt guid, is pronounced more as 'geed' in Galloway and 'gid' in Dumfries (generally). The Galloway 'l' (el) is pronounced with the tongue right back similar to French. In Scots, most vowel sounds are short so that 'moon' becomes more like 'min' and would be spelt 'muin' – 'sin an muin'. Any word with 'ui', 'guid', is 'oo' (good) or sometimes 'oul' (could) in English. Words such as night become nicht with the 'ch' sounded as in loch. The syntax is usually similar but not always; sometimes it is similar to early nineteenth-century English. In the past, words that apparently ended in 'ing' were often written, even by Robert Burns, as in' with a comma to suggest the missing 'g'. In fact, the 'g' is an addition in the southern English dialect. The 'g' never was there so the comma is redundant – similarly, German verbs often end in 'en' not 'eng'. In the South-West of Scotland many words do not have an end letter, for example, 'aroon' instead of 'around' or 'an' instead of 'and'. Verbs ending in 'ed' as in 'thanked' in Scots end in 'it', with an equal stress on the ending as in 'thankit', for example, 'the soun o twa hauns clappit' = the sound of two hands clapped.

Aa	all
Aamichty	almighty
Ablow	below
Abuin	above
Ae, yae, yin, wan	a or one
Agin	against
Ahint	behind
Aiblins	perhaps
Ain	own
Antrin	strange, odd
Auld	old
Auld Cluitie, Auld Hornie, Auld Nick, the Deil	the Devil
Ava	at all
Aye	yes
Aye	forever
Bairn	child
Bannock	baked bread made from barley or oats
Bannockstane	a flat stone for baking
Bànrigh na Sìthichean	(gaelic) Queen of the Fairies
Bauchan	a dangerous hobgoblin that, on occasions, can be helpful
Bawbee	six pence Scots
Begunkit	cheated or deceived
Beir	to bear, carry
Ben	the living area of the house – 'come ben the hoose'
Birlinn	similar to a Viking longboat
Bittie	small bit
Bogle	hobgoblin
Bothy	hut or small cottage
Brammle	bramble, blackberry

Braw	splendid, fine
Breeks	breeches, trousers cut off below the knee
Brocht	brought
Brose	boiled barley, butter and salt
Brou	brow
Brownie	(broonie) a good-natured elf-like creature that helps with the chores
Bucht	sheep pen
Burn	stream
Byordinar	extraordinary
Byre	cowshed
Caa	call
Cadger	pedlar or hawker
Cannie	wise
Cannywife	midwife (see also 'howdie')
Cantrip	magic spell
Cappy	wooden bowl
Carlin	witch, originally a woman (from the Norse)
Caudron	cauldron
Caunle	candle
Ceilidh	gathering, party
Chalmer of dais	(chamber of the high table) parlour
Changelin	changeling, a strange, fairy child left in place of a human child
Chiel	fellow
Clachan	(gaelic) village
Cleekit	hooked
Clew	ball (of wool)
Cley	clay
Coggie	wooden bowl
Contramawcious	obstinate
Convicta et combusta	convicted and burned
Coo	cow
Cot	cottage

Cotillion	French courtly dance for four couples
Coulter	cutter on a plough
Coupit	pushed over
Craik	neck
Creel	wicker basket for carrying on the back or to use as a fish trap
Craitur	creature
Crony	companion
Cruisie	oil lamp
Dae	do
Daith	death
Daoine Sith	(gaelic) (deena shee) faery folk
Darg	work, a day's work
Daunce	dance
Daur	dare
Daurk	dark
Deid	dead
Deif	deaf
Deil	devil
Diablerie	the Devil's work
Dinnae	do not
Disnae	does not
Doon	down
Dowie	sad
Druid	pagan priest
Een	even
Een	eyes
Eldritch	unearthly, weird
Eleivin	eleven
Eneuch	enough
Episcopalian	church organised under bishops
Etherstane	(adderstone) prehistoric holed stone used as a charm or talisman
Fand	found
Fankle	a tangle, predicament

Fash	trouble, agitate
Faulds	fields
Feart	frightened
Fecht	fight
Fellthocht	reconsider
Ferlie	a wonder
Fleetch	flatter
Forgie	forgive
Flyte	scold
Forfochtan	tired out
Forgieness	forgiveness
Fou, fuu	full
Frae	from
Gait	road
Gang	go
Garron	small sturdy Scottish pony
Gaunnae	going to
Gear	property
Gett	abusive name for a child
Gey	very, a great quantity
Gie	give
Giftie	present
Gin	if or whether
Girdle	griddle, a flat metal plate for baking bread, scones oatkes and bannocks on
Glaistig	half woman, half goat; fond of helping to look after cattle, though sometimes acquires a taste for human blood
Glamour	enchantment
Glebe	agricultural land belong to the church
Gloamin	twilight
Gowd	gold
Grespit	grasped
Greetin	crying
Guager	tax collector

Guidman	husband
Guidneichbour	(good neighbour) fairy folk
Guidwife	housewife
Guises	disguises
Gyte	foolish
Hae	have
Haud	hold
Haund, haun	hand
Hecht	promise
Heich	high
Hen	term of endearment
Howdie	midwife
Hurl	lift in a vehicle
I	(lower case i) in
Ilka	each, every
Ingine	intelligence
Ingle	fire
Ingleneuk	inset seat in a fireplace
Intil	into
Itherwarld	otherworld
Jade/jad	ill-tempered woman
Jalouse	suspect
Jiggert	damaged, broken
Jouk	swerve round, avoid
Jyne	join
Kane	rent or fee
Keek	peek, look
Ken	know
Kentna	knew not
Kintra-fowk	country folk
Kirk	church
Knockingstane	stone for grinding flour
Laird	landowner when not of the aristocracy
Lea	leave
Loss	lose

Loup	leap
Lue	love
Luesome	loving
Lum	chimney
Mair	more
Maiter	matter
Mannie	little or young man
Mauken	hare
Maun	must
Maut	malt (for whisky)
Meat	a meal, food in general, meat
Meenit	minute
Mercat	market
Metalled	hard-packed stone road
Micht	might
Mirk	dusk, dark
Moond	mound
Moul	a chilblain
Muckle	great
Mutch	linen bonnet
Mynd	remember, concerned
Myrmidons	a follower, originally one of the followers of the Greek hero, Achilles
Nae	not, no
Nane	none
Nocht	nothing
Nowt	nothing
Ower	over
Owerburthint	overburdened
Pairt	part
Peat, peit	decayed vegetable matter dug up, dried and used as fuel
Pelf	possessions
Pey	pay
Pickle	small amount

Pinnie	pinafore
Pooer	power
Pootch	pouch, pocket
Pownie	pony
Preasse	attack
Preens	pins
Prentice	apprentice
Presbyterian	church run by ministers and elders
Puu	pull
Quaich	a shallow drinking bowl
Rashes	(bull)rushes
Reel	frame for winding yarn
Reeve	tear
Riddle	a rough sieve for sifting soil or sand
Rime	frost
Ryal	royal
Sacbaun	a wraith that appears in a shroud, similar to a banshee
Sairy	sorry
Sark	shirt
Saul	soul
Scant	in short supply
Schuilin	schooling
Shellycoat	river creature similar to a brownie but fond of playing tricks
Shoon	shoes
Shilpit	skinny
Shirramuir	Battle of Sherriffmuir in the first Jacobite rebellion on 13 November 1715
Sic	such
Siccar	sure, certain
Siller	silver
Sìth/sìdhe	(gaelic) (pronounced shee) faeries or elves
Sìth-mara	sea elves
Sìthbheire	(gaelic) (sheevera) see 'changeling'

Skein	a length of yarn wound on a reel
Skirlin	screeching
Smeddum	spirit, mettle
Smiddy	smithy, a blacksmith's workshop
Sneck	door-latch
Snood	woman's headband
Socht	sought, searched for
Sook	suck
Spate	high water, flood
Spring	tune
Stang	(ride the stang) punishment by riding on a pole and being beaten and abused
Sterne	star
Suir	sure
Taen	taken
Teaslin	teasing
Theik	thatch
Thulmart (foul martin)	polecat
Tine	the prong on a harrow, rake or fork
Tint	lost
Touer	tower
Tow	unspun flax
Tryst	meeting
Twalmonth	twelve months/a year
Unco	very, strangely, rare
Unyirthly	unearthly
Veesit	visit
Wat	wet
Waur	worse
Weans	(little ones) children
Weel	well
Wert	were
Wheels	wheels of Hell
Wheesht	quiet

Whiles	sometimes
Whin	gorse bush
Wicht	creature, usually supernatural
Wid	wood
Wile	entrap, cunning
Winding-sheet	a long sheet to wrap a dead body
Wit	sense, to think or reason
Wraith	ghost, often dangerous
Wrocht	wrought; made
Wytins	accusations
Yirth	Earth
Yonner	yonder
Yowe	ewe, sheep

Scottish Storytelling Forum

The Scottish Storytelling Centre is delighted to be associated with the *Folk Tales* series developed by The History Press. Its talented storytellers continue the Scottish tradition, revealing the regional riches of Scotland in these volumes. These include the different environments, languages and cultures encompassed in our big wee country. The Scottish Storytelling Centre provides a base and communications point for the national storytelling network, along with national networks for Traditional Music and Song and Traditions of Dance, all under the umbrella of TRACS (Traditional Arts and Culture Scotland). See www.scottishstorytellingcentre.co.uk for further information. The Traditional Arts community of Scotland is also delighted to be working with all the nations and regions of Great Britain and Ireland through the *Folk Tales* series.